C000132469

WHO AM I IN THE WORLD?

WHO AM I IN THE WORLD?

A STORY OF BECOMING

Rowena Marin

NEW DEGREE PRESS

COPYRIGHT © 2023 ROWENA MARIN

All rights reserved.

WHO AM I IN THE WORLD?

A Story of Becoming

ISBN

979-8-88926-635-8 *Paperback*

979-8-88926-634-1 *eBook*

to my mother, my rock.

to my daughter, may you learn to become who you are.

to my husband, my heart.

to my siblings, I learned what love is from the three of you.

to my community, I would not be who I am if not for all of you.

to my daughters, may you light up the world.

Contents

Drawing upon your deepest resources,
You shall overcome all difficulties
Through my grace. But if you will heed me
In your self-will, nothing will avail you.
If you say, "I will not fight this battle,"
Your own nature will drive you into it.
If you will not fight the battle of life,
Your own karma will drive you into it.

—SRI KRISHNA,
THE BHAGAVAD GITA, BE AWARE OF ME ALWAYS

A Letter to My Daughters

Dear Daughters,

This letter comes to you from a long line of brave and daring Romani women. You are the fruit of all of us, and I want you to learn the lessons of life passed down to me as I have learned and unlearned them to become who you see today.

You are part of a very special community, probably the only ethnic group in the world with more than twelve million people spread across the continents, with no country of our own. We are the Romani people, and that is what others should call us. Your grandmother never called us anything but *Gypsies*, but that was her right and now mine. We originated in Northern India and fled to Europe and the Americas many centuries ago, looking for a better life. We fled in small groups, each defined by their work. You and I come from a jewelry-making community, so we are called *Argintari* or the *Silverers*.

Life was probably good for your ancestors in Romania until one day, the country's Boyars (the nobles) decided to make us all slaves. So, you are a descendant of a family of slaves. I hope you will love meeting your great-great-grandmother in the first part of this book. She survived slavery and the abject poverty that came with liberation to raise many children, nephews, and nieces. Children that fought during World War I, nephews, and nieces that survived the concentration camps during World War II. Because you see, we are survivors. We make it against all odds, defy social norms, and remain a close family despite all the challenges through the two things that truly unite us: the love and respect we have for each other.

Like any other family, we can also be evil to each other. And just like any other closed community, some of our antiquated norms, which mostly affect women, hurt our growth and our future. I wanted you to know all these layers of your extended family so you can truly understand your roots. Life has not been all peaches and cream for any member of our community, including myself. However, in the next chapters, you will see how the hardships became a fire that molded us into resilient, creative, adaptable, and caring human beings.

You will find in the book stories about growing up, mother-daughter relationships, loss and grief, self-discovery, brotherhood, sisterhood, friendship, and success. Along the way, I have made many mistakes, hurt people, lost myself, and lied, but my biggest mistake was to be inauthentic to please others. I try to forgive myself, accept all my layers, and do a better job in my present life, where I give myself to people around me that I love.

You see, the most surprising thing I learned in my journey to discovering who I am was that after finding authenticity and acceptance, all I wanted to do was lose myself to my loved ones. The biggest power and fulfillment I ever found was in unconditional love, but this beautiful fruit doesn't blossom in a closed heart. As your uncle Raymond taught me, "the most difficult journey in life is going from the mind to the heart."

For many years, as you will read, I was living in an illusion, trying to fit into molds that either our community or the society we lived in had created, so my heart was far from open. I didn't know better because one can't ever know what a mountain smells like until one gets there. But to get there, they have to take the journey because the mountain doesn't come to you. When you don't know yourself, you allow others to hurt you, and sometimes the people you love most are the ones that hurt you beyond repair. That is what happened to me, and I want you to learn this so that with your creativity and resourcefulness, you will know better than to let anyone tell you who you are or hurt you, even if they love you. Forgive them if they try by understanding and seeing the fear behind their actions, but don't allow their fear to define you.

If you ever ask yourself who you are in this big world you are part of, know the answer is in the journey you dare to take, and the key you always need to keep in your heart is courage. The same courage helped me start the journey myself, as you will read in the next chapters. Although you might feel lonely along the way, know that you are never alone.

Don't ever pass by someone in trouble and not stop to help. Never judge someone else only by appearance. Don't whine, keep your head high, and have faith. Trust in yourself and others around you, but be smart and distinguish between purely maleficent people and those who are scared of your power. Scared people tend to try to put you down, discriminate against you, talk behind your back, or make you doubt yourself. Don't make any space for such people. If they are in your family, pray for them, but stay away.

Stand tall, as God favors the brave ones, not the ones who don't make any mistakes. Learn your lessons, grow, create opportunities around you, and be humble. But most importantly, know that you do not owe anything to anyone. Your only duty is to be truly alive and leave this world just a little bit better than when you came into it.

Standing on the shoulders of your ancestors, learn about this mighty race of Gypsies, as many lessons can help you on your journey. Once you finish this book, take your courage, wear it like a second skin, and dare to become who you are.

A girl who became a woman,
Rowena

PART ONE
THE FAMILY

CHAPTER 1

Gypsy Dinner

Romania, 1993

Our house is an oven. My father and his cousins, my siblings, and our cousins—we are dizzy. July is too hot in Bucharest, and we are hungry. We are waiting for Grandma Gutuia to finish, as she has been cooking since noon. Watch the yellow walls as they melt in the sun coming in through the place where the window of our broken front door used to be. Watch the steam coming out of the tiny kitchen on Siminocului Street, where Grandma is making beaten beans and bread, her son's favorite.

My mother, Buna, spends all morning at the flea market, selling silver rings handmade by my dad—Harry. Gutuia waits for my mother to come back home with the ingredients. The Gypsy version of my grandmother's food is different from the one made by Romanians. She spends many hours choosing the perfect beans, washing them at least ten times, and then boiling them forever. She even makes the bread differently. Ours is round, flat, and white, whereas theirs is brown, fluffy, and full.

Smell the comfort of knowing hunger will vanish together with the last piece of dough transforming right now in our brick-improvised stove. Let the heat sink any desire you might have for your own space. In this house, space is a luxury we cannot afford. Our bodies are so close to each other, sitting on the carpets, that we can almost hear our thoughts.

Listen to the sound of pots, pans, knives, and harsh directions my mother receives, between the kitchen's hot four walls, from her mother-in-law. She wouldn't dare do anything other than obey, especially in front of the family.

Laugh at the misplaced jokes the men make, forgetful of the fact that the children's improvised table sits just beside their round carpet, used as a table. We find ourselves taken away by the laughter, the feelings, the comments, the unspoken rules, or the novelty of never knowing what the day will bring.

Even my father's half brother, Ion, appears unwanted to join the men, intentionally forgetting to greet his stepmother properly.

"*Avilean* (You came)?" said Gutuia in the only tongue she likes to speak, our Romani language.

"*Avileas* (He came)," answered my dad for his half brother.

He came to eat beaten beans and bread. My mom's sister, Madama, disfigured by her wrinkles but always with a red headband covering her hair, stumbles through the door frame. She is also dizzy and hungry.

"*Dobroiptumenga* (Hello)," she greets. The kids laugh. The men greet. The other women put her to work. Everyone but the men are preparing one meal.

"Sergiu, come here," said my uncle Udila, one of the men sitting at the carpet-table, to his son, one year younger than me.

"Tell all of them who is the strongest boy in the world."

"I am," said Sergiu victoriously, while showing his skinny arms to everyone.

His older sister, my cousin Ramona, cries to her mother, her tears reaching her chest, and says, "Both of you only love my brother, not me."

Her mother doesn't even blink at the statement and continues to work in the kitchen with the women. We all are restless, not finding our place to sit.

"Just a little bit more," I say, trying to conceal the sound of my stomach. "Let's all wait just a little bit more," I say again, comforting Ramona, whose cries pierced our ears.

The one who always got everything she wanted is now the victim. Delia, Ramona's little sister, is pounding her feet on the ground to test the music-making sandals she just got a few days ago. Bianca, another cousin my age, is playing catch by herself, running from our carpet-table to the small yard in front of the house and tapping each one of us hard every time she comes back.

My sister Loredana, although eleven years old, is playing with a spinning top that makes a weird sound she likes to imitate on higher and higher notes. Our two brothers, Lucian and Raymond, who are in their early twenties, get to sit with the men.

All the boys my age are silent, eavesdropping on what their fathers and uncles are discussing a few inches away from them. They want to become men as soon as possible.

The family has too many children, and I am one of them. I blend in perfectly between my three siblings and my twenty-plus cousins, just like the fringes on a carpet. We resemble each other, we eat as one, we play as one, slight differences you will only encounter when you switch to a different age group. But put my five-year-old self at the same table or the same movie with the others, and we will eat or sob in harmony.

I have my father's patience, my mother's acceptance, my grandma's drive, my uncle's courage, and my aunt's thick skin. I learned from being a fly on the wall, listening. My name is distinctive. Rare in the world and unique among my people. My father wanted everyone to call me Rowena. The Romani people do not go by their names. They sometimes even forget it. My father Harry was Niculae, my mother Buna was Ileana, and Grandma Gutuia was really... I don't even know. I was lucky. I am named after the princess in *Ivanhoe*. But I was a princess only for my father. Otherwise, I am one among many. Unique only by the name.

The food is ready. The women yell from the steamy kitchen oven, "Rowena, Loredana, Ramona, Bianca, Delia, come serve."

We rush in, Delia's tiny shoes singing a jolly song. We grab the plates that are bigger than our heads. We never use cutlery. I am not sure we even have forks. We rush to the round carpet. We serve the men. My hands are too small to grab the plate well, so I barely make it in one piece. I want to dip a finger and taste it, but I am afraid I won't be able to stop. Someone new appears through our brown door. It's Carmen, one of my older cousins.

"Mother, I heard you made bread and beans, and you called for me," she says.

Both Gutuia and my mom answer almost in one voice, "Yes, sit down!"

We do not speak. We are all still waiting for the men to finish eating. Even my sister's loud voice is silent. Our minds are melting to the floor. We wait.

After eternity passed, my mom, grandma, and Madama brought us kids a big bowl of Gypsy dinner. The women remain in their hot kitchen. I know my mom is hungry. She was out all day to bring Grandma the beans and the flour to cook. I hope she starts eating soon. My heart cries for her, but my stomach was crying a long time before my heart, so I indulge in my favorite dish.

The thickness and warmth of the bread, melting in the sauce of the beans calms us all down, putting a smile on everyone's face. I can perceive the men's voices now talking more calmly. Bianca stopped running, Delia stopped pounding, Ramona stopped crying, and bliss is the state we all found ourselves in.

Close your eyes and let this feeling sink in, as it will be the through-line of this story of becoming. We, the Romani people, although toughened by life and the rules we created for ourselves to survive centuries of oppression, support each other unconditionally. This support allowed me to grow wings, fly away, and come back. I invite you on this journey. Take a seat at our children's table and come along.

CHAPTER 2

The Singer Slave

How can I show you the world of the once enslaved Romani people since I was spared just by the pure luck of being born a century later? I have no choice but to walk you through the streets of the memories of my great-grandmother, Manole Cristina or Ristina—the only name she would call herself. Although we never met, her stories have been passed down from generation to generation, only to spark the imagination of my inquiring mind in 2020.

Let's take the year 1886, when she turned fourteen: Twenty-one years after slavery was abolished in the US, the same year that the Spanish government abolished slavery in Cuba, and thirty years since the abolishment of Roma slavery in the Romanian Principalities of Moldova and Walachia.

Sit down with me on the edge of this grain field while the sun is showing its first rays. Hear the rooster's sharp wake-up call and smell the earthy chills of the morning.

Right across this field, bordering the city of Alexandria, Teleorman, in Romania, you will see the shack where Ristina and her husband live. It's sitting exactly in the middle of a row of homemade shacks made out of pieces from abandoned houses, covered with posts, cardboard, corrugated metal, and pieces of cloth, together with some real windows and some improvised ones made of nylon.

She lights a candle for us and gets out of the space where she sleeps: a patched piece of wood that serves as a bed. She puts on a long piece of gray cloth over the other gray cloth she is already wearing. She ties her thick, long hair, black as a shield against sunshine. The sun is just showing itself little by little, offering the chance to see herself in the piece of mirror hanging from the entrance door. We see her better now as the sunlight intensifies. Her head tilted to the side, where the hair spouts like water. Her big black eyes can brighten up your soul. She is mumbling something while her ebony lashes are waving at us from the mirror's reflection. She is thin, tall, and white-skinned with childlike cheeks.

We can almost hear her husband firmly nudging her to rush out as they need to leave for work. Married just a year before, they are still learning to be a couple, although he is much older than her. Serban, or *the ugly one* as the silversmith community called Ristina's husband, chose her for her beauty, although the youngest one among the three sisters. Her parents were happy to give him their daughter because he was known for being hard-working, patient, and honorable.

We follow them out on the street. You will notice her gaze looking down all the time, as her husband leads the way a few feet ahead of her. Although spring, you can feel the cold piercing through your bones with every wind blow. A short boot loosely fits her left foot, and her right foot sits in a black shoe.

The little street line is now teeming with people, all dressed in the same piece of gray cloth, a few wearing some sort of hardened brown leather jacket on top and most barefoot. They will pass that strip of land, leave behind their homes, cross a country road, and arrive at their daily destination: the land of the *Boyard*, the landlord of all those grain fields.

Ristina is not a slave in papers, but her landlord still owns her. She does not know another way of existing, as she is the fruit of the love of two Gypsy slaves who continued to work in these fields until the day they died. That's the same reason you see this flock of silversmith Romani people working in this field from dawn to sunset, planting, seeding, pruning, harvesting crops, and packing them for shipment. Before being enslaved, silversmiths were masters of jewelry making, but right now, they are tools owned by a *Boyard*.

You might as well ask what is Ristina thinking, while her body is crouched down to the ground, trying to pluck all the weeds around the grains. Does she have any intuition that freedom is so close, just a generation away? Perhaps she is hungry, and all she can think about is the meal coming up at the end of the workday. Perhaps she is scared of lifting her body up to see the sky because they told her the enslaver has his eyes on her.

"No one can save a woman when the landlord wants you," they say.

Maybe all that, or maybe none.

One thing is for sure: she is singing. If you listen carefully, you can hear the melody or the one song passed down to me and you: *Seven mouths to feed with a bitter bread.*

The melody is soothing for her and others around her who listen, although the words are harsh, as they speak of a time of famine and sorrow.

The song speaks about the lives of many generations and many souls whose stories have been buried by history, especially in Romania, where slavery was a topic excluded from the books of history.

I have tried to search for this song, but even with all the technology we have in the twenty-first century, I haven't found it. I wish I could hum the melody here on this paper to portray the deep sadness it provokes in my heart when I remember it.

The way it got to me was through my aunt Matilda. Ristina raised Aunt Matilda and was in her nineties when she died. My aunt is now seventy-three. Only through the chance created by the pandemic I moved back in with my mother for a few months. My aunt stayed with us, and I got the chance to hear this song for the first time. She sang the refrain in a low voice while watching a Turkish soap opera with my mother.

I asked, "What is this song about?" That's how the stories began.

In the early 1900s, when the *Boyard* lost his lands, Ristina, her husband, and five children were finally free but uneducated, with no idea what they could do with their lives. So she started singing on the streets and begging for food. Her voice echoed on every street in Alexandria, Romania, day in and day out, and wealthier women would give her flour, potatoes, eggs, and whatever else they could spare.

This is how she raised her children and some of her nieces, including my aunt Matilda. This is how she got through the years of World War II after the deportation of her husband and children to Transnistria. She continued singing her sorrow and making it day by day with the only real dream of surviving the week, the month, and the year, together with her family.

"Was she ever happy?" I asked my mom and Aunt Matilda.

"Sometimes, after the long days of work, all our people would gather to sing. Because she had the most beautiful voice, everyone would gather in front of their house, start a fire, and spend the entire night telling stories, singing, and dancing. That's what got them through the pain and sorrow," my aunt said.

"That's how we did it also. When times were difficult, we came together as a family," my mother said.

"After the war, when they sent our people back from Transnistria, Ristina convinced the local authorities to give her a place to live for her, her children, and her nephews because her eldest son, my grandfather, fought and was injured. She was the only Gypsy in town to have a place to live. Therefore, many of our people had a place to stay, in her backyard, while they figured out life again," mother continued.

Ristina (great-great-grandmother)

MY LETTER TO RISTINA:
How can I reach you? I've been singing your song for days now, waking up in the middle of the night, my mind humming away without me, calling you. Speak to me. I am singing to go back to the time before you gave birth to us when you were just a girl sitting in the frame of the door, looking at the sky, singing in Alexandria, Romania, 1886.

The melody of your song haunts my sleep, and it's becoming almost unbearable because the words won't come to me. They are right there but never arrive on my lips. All I have are these six words of the refrain: "Seven people and a bitter bread" and a melody waiting for me to complete. I imagine those seven people, and all I can see is a dog gnawing on a piece of bread. We live in a world so different from yours, where people are free to travel everywhere they can dream of, where we talk about freedom of speech, equality, and racial justice. Of course, we are far from a world where these ideals are the experience of everyone. But we are also far from your world, where they enslaved you and your family.

At the Romanian Orthodox Church in New York, where I live now, there are no Gypsies at the Sunday mass. Everyone is Romanian and proper. I stand taller, raise my shoulders, and breathe in deeply as I walk through the gate. As soon as I enter, my gaze drops to the ground, and my back hunches again. I make no eye contact as I try to find a seat or a place to stand, surrounded by no one. When I pray for hours on my mat at home, I experience the same peace as when I see the sunrise. At church, I hear all the sounds simultaneously, cluttering, stacking on top of each other, my heart pumping faster and faster until I find my place.

Some days, instead of hiding in a spot far removed from everyone, I find myself taking two seats: one for my body and another for my expensive jacket and purse. I try not to take the purse with me to Queens, but something inside me associates safety with showing status.

"Maybe they will believe I am one of them if I wear these items," a voice whispers in my head.

The other day I decided to take the two seats and even sit cross-legged, which is not allowed, according to an older woman. My eyes focus on the painting of Saint Mary, my heart pumping, my hands shaking. I sit there for three hours, breathing.

When the service ends, as I am getting ready to leave as fast as possible, a woman stops and compliments me on my eyes. I look into her eyes and remember your song then and there. My mind just grips the words, and I feel weak. I sit down to catch my breath and wonder if you want me to forgive these people for enslaving you. They left you with nothing but a song to sing when *the church* gave up slavery in Romania, as they were enslavers too. As you know, it took us three generations to climb out of absolute poverty and shame, either on the outskirts of society or in prison, and finally start thriving. Some of us still live in the imprisonment of our minds.

Walk with me back home from church on this cold day in February in New York. Today, five years ago, I started working for a company that helped me take the leap from a life of day-to-day survival to living a decent life where you don't count every penny when you buy food, you don't suffer for your children's hunger, and where you can give to others.

But that was a long journey, Great-Grandma. It took us 136 years.

CHAPTER 3
Women That Kneel

From high up, where you can take aerial photographs, the horseshoe-shaped Potcoavei Street in Alexandria, Teleorman, Romania, is hardly even a minuscule spot. In satellite images shot from a higher still, the street of the Gypsies is just a figment of your imagination.

If you descend to the ground level, your feet on the city's dirt roads, and if you know what to look for, you might be able to see Cosilda's golden tooth.

Dark-skinned and short, the teenager just found love and is running to her cousin's house, her neighbor, to tell her the latest news. Cosilda is fifteen in 1947 and lives in one of the hardened mud houses on the street. One wrong left from the main road, beyond the three craters in the ground created by the rain, you will find a place with a loud group of children playing hide-and-go-seek, a group of older men enjoying the sun, and a group of older women chatting.

Cosilda salutes the elder for the third time today, showing her shiny smile and then running inside her yard. There is only a see-through small fence between her shack and her cousin's. She touches the fence with one hand, vaults her legs and long skirt across, and is already at the destination. She covers her dirty ankles quickly and finds her beloved cousin Fahalda.

See them joining both hands above their hearts in excitement, running outside, on Potcoava and further even, to the main road, where no one else can hear them.

"So penel chio Dad, chi Dei (What will your father and mother say)?" asks Fahalda, looking down at her toes.

"Oste naseau lesa (I am going to run with him)," bursts out Cosilda.

Running with a boy one loves means making love to him, and making love with a boy means marriage for life in the silversmith Gypsy community.

"Samanga dar (I'm afraid)," we hear Fahada whispering.

"Manga naimaga (I'm not)!" responds Cosilda.

See them returning to the street where Cosilda's brother is waiting for her, his foot dancing by itself, up and down like a ticking bomb. She jumps into his arms, dissembling the bomb. He reaches across her body, and with her still hanging, he takes her back inside their yard.

"S ireat se, naituca dar ca te cioren (It's late, I am afraid some boy will steal you)," he said.

Cosilda smiles at her brother and turns to take the broom and starts cleaning the kitchen floor. "To be stolen" means that a man rapes a girl or a woman into marriage.

Late at night, Cosilda sneaks out of the house, crosses the street, crosses the main road, and takes a turn on the second street. Armand waits for her with a rose. He stood barefoot in the dimmed light, with a gray shirt and black trousers. His face lights up, and he blushes as she approaches. Her long green dress, covered in dust from sweeping the floor, resembles a ball dress in the night light.

Both constantly look left and right, checking for any sounds or signs of danger. Armand hugs Cosilda tightly and gives her the flower, kissing her right cheek twice.

"Armand, my parents will never allow me to marry you. What do we do?" she asks while playing with her flower.

He touches her hands to stop her and replies gently, "We run, we run next week. You are mine, and I am yours," he says, his teenage voice cracking.

She wraps her arms around his neck. He picks her up and stops his lips one inch far from her lips. He puts her back down and takes her hand. He takes her back, close to the entrance of the hidden street, and watches as she slips inside her little gate. He continues the journey to the other end of the street and walks into the dark alley in front of his home, avoiding the three craters and into his yard.

Meanwhile, Cosilda is waiting below her windowless window for the signal. As soon as she hears the snore of her youngest sister Gutuia three times, she sneaks in and crawls into the bed where her mother and sisters are sleeping. As soon as her heart stops drumming, she hugs Gutuia tightly and whispers to herself.

"Run, I will run, we will run away."

She sighs one more time, and two more words fall from her mouth: run, run.

The morning starts before the sun is up.

"No!" she screams as she fights a huge blanket off her face her mother had thrown to wake her up.

"Yes! Come on, faster, before your father gets up. Let's go," her mother says.

She wakes up to an empty bed, all her siblings dressed and ready to go. She jumps out of bed, heads to the kitchen, bumps her head hard on the ready-to-fall cabinet door, takes a bottle of water, and pours it on her face.

"I'm awake. Let's go," Cosilda mumbles.

She puts on another shirt while trying to catch up with her family already outside. As they head out, the cats and dogs of the neighborhood are the only ones to greet them. The houses of all their neighbors look empty.

They make their way out on the main road, where they find the first lights, and we can finally see them all together. All of them were thin, tall people, except for Cosilda, who, for some reason, just did not grow as much as the others. She looks like the baby of the family, although Gutuia is. The brothers are the only ones with shoes on, and the parents both have gray hair. They keep close and move slowly as a unit. They make it to the night bus station that appears after a few minutes of walking. They each take a place, two by two. Cosilda takes the seat close to her mother, facing the window.

"I had a bad dream, Mom. I don't know, I'm afraid," she tells her mother.

Eyes closed and head falling over, her mother mumbles, "Me too. Tell me yours."

Looking at the dark streets disappearing one by one, Cosilda lets out a sigh and says, "I was a small pebble close to the moon. I asked the moon something, but I can't remember what. She didn't want to answer and looked away, upset. Then I grew black roots which were pulling me down in the earth, away from her. I fought so much to stay close to her warmth, love, and light, but the roots were stronger and bigger than me. I asked for her help, but she couldn't do anything. Her half face was disappearing more and more, and I got pulled like a horse into the mud," she stopped to see her mother sleeping, face down, hands down, melting into the seat.

After almost three hours, they arrive in Bucharest, the place they would come to a few times a week to either sell jewelry or trade-in jewelry for food. They spread into pairs of two and start walking on each street. Cosilda pairs with her eldest brother. They arrive at the first house and ring the bell. A Romanian lady opens the gate.

"Mother, we have rings and other jewelry and are searching for food. Would you want to see what we have?" Cosilda says.

The lady lets them in and shows them to the backyard. She brings pastry and water and looks at each ring closely, trying on different models. She takes two, one for her and one for her husband, and offers them a few kilograms of flour, cheese, eggs, and even a few dimes. They continue like this the entire day, after which they have their bags full of food. It was a successful day, so they decided to head back to the bus station—the meeting point for everyone. They arrive, but the rest of the family is still not there.

"Let's wait for them at the bus station bar. We have money to buy water," Cosilda says.

Her brother joyfully nods and takes the bags off the ground to follow her. They find a table in the shade, order the water, and sit down to wait for the family.

"I'm going to use the bathroom, don't move," she says.

Her brother nods in agreement while taking the first sip of the cold water. She finds her way to the public bathrooms, behind the bar, and down the alley, and lifts her skirt while closing the door in a rush. But the door doesn't close because someone is holding it. A man grabs the back of her shirt and her hair and pulls her out, making her fall and hit her head. She faints.

Now surrounded by four young men, all a bit older than her, she screams, "Leave me alone, please!"

They all start laughing at her as she covers her legs with her skirt, fighting the pain in her forehead.

"You will be my wife, whether you like it or not," says Rudy, the tallest of the men.

"Go away, I beg you!" Cosilda says again.

Rudy's youngest brother grabs her hair and smacks her head against the massive tree she is leaning against.

"Stop it!" shouts Rudy. "I don't want a broken wife. I want her in one piece. Now let me handle this. You hold her," he commands to the other three.

Each of them grabs a limb, the elder grabs her left leg, the short one grabs her left hand, the fat one grabs her right leg, and he digs his dirty nails into her right shoulder. The elder one lifts her skirt up to make way for Rudy and gives him the white towel.

Rudy lays the white towel under Cosilda and whispers: "Don't fight it. Give in to me."

The tears flooding her face, neck, and chest sound deaf under Rudy's left hand, which covers her mouth while he unbuttons his pants. Her green pupils bury deeply in her eye sockets. The white towel is now red. The men laugh and rejoice. Rudy is now married.

They take her numb body and put it into the carriage, waiting for them nearby. Rudy sits her on a bed of leaves in the carriage and starts his way back home.

Cosilda's family is searching for her everywhere. Has anyone seen her, they ask. Has anyone seen a short girl with a long-braided tail in a long skirt, green eyes, and brown skin? But no one has.

"Oh, someone took her," the mother screams.

"It's my fault!" says the elder brother. "I should have gone with her to the bathroom."

"Let's go to Rudy's family and check she is not there," said the father, who knew this family wanted his daughter.

Late in the night, they arrive. They open the door and hear music and people dancing. The mother faints.

"Where is my daughter?" asks Cosilda's father to the crowd gathered in Rudy's backyard to celebrate the occasion.

Rudy's father greets him, "Welcome, my new brother. Now we are forever relatives. My son has chosen your daughter and married her today," he said.

His blood pops directly into his eyes, filling them with stains of red and yellow. He wipes off his tears with the back of his fists and approaches Rudy, who is bringing the white/red towel.

"She was a virgin, my wife," he shouts with all the strength of his lungs. "She is mine!"

Cosilda's mother and sisters run into the house to find her. Her brothers and father stay outside, with the others, to discuss arrangements. Cosilda, now dressed in white, kneels alongside the bed.

"I'm here," her mother whispers in her ear.

"Come back home, Cosilda," says Gutuia, hugging her sister.

Cosilda reacts by stabbing her mother's arm with her nails.

"Take me home!" she says without blinking.

Her mother's eyes descend to hell, knowing she can't. Her daughter Cosilda is a married woman and has to stay there.

Her father slams the door open and declares calmly, "We take her home."

Not a virgin anymore, Armand could never marry her. Cosilda died in her bed six months after. They say it was due to a broken heart.

CHAPTER 4

The Good One—Buna

My good one, because I am your daughter, what I know of work, I know equally of loss of oneself. And what I know of both, I know of your silence. The smoke coming out of your mouth instead of words every time I ask you about your life before getting married says everything. What I know of work is sacrificing yourself for your family and your community, giving up on your dreams to follow the way given to you: traveling from one place to another to sell or trade items handmade by the men in the family. These journeys from one flea market to another, from village to village, from city to city, in buses, cars, and trains, were not just journeys but a way of life where you raised all four of us and a dozen other children not born to you, and still yours. In the blazing Sun, the unforgiving Romanian winters or icy rains, the fairs and flea markets were a place of folklore, rumors, tales, and jokes where you learned what life is and taught us all.

I hate and love your silence, knowing it made me who I am today, and it tells the story of your life.

The year is 1970. Costica's daughter, my mother Buna (in Romanian—the good one), is twenty-one. While *Apollo*

13 was failing its landing on the moon, Buna was home in Hotvon—one of the slums three kilometers away from the city, dedicated to the Gypsies, located nearby the city of Baia Mare, Romania. She was the youngest daughter of Costica and Niculina and the sister of Ion, Boi, Madama, and Filica.

Sit down with me on the abandoned railway line, where you can see all the twenty-four houses that make up the neighborhood. We are sitting right in front of Buna's house. She is wearing a long, colorful skirt and a yellow top and brushing her thick, long hair. She pauses a moment as if she just remembered something and runs to the back of the house, where she soaks some dirty laundry in water. We follow Buna with our eyes to the back of the house, where her father left one big tank of water so women can use it to wash clothes. She also has two basins, one red and another one black. The red one is used to wash the clothes with detergent, and the black one is for rinsing. Close to the basin is also a stool to sit on while washing. The stool is for the elder women who visit. Young women are not supposed to use it while washing, as it can signify laziness. She takes the red basin, adds water, and sinks in all the dirty laundry, adding a little packet of detergent, then takes the basin and sits it on top of the stool. The skin on her porcelain white hands becomes red in a matter of minutes due to the scrubbing and the cold water. Her fingers are long and perfectly balanced with her nails. Each nail bed is a dream for a manicurist. When she finishes with one piece of clothing, she tosses it into the black basin.

As she continues this dance with the dirty laundry, a family approaches their house. It's one of Costica's brothers—Dinu, his wife, and his children. Even though the house shouldn't accommodate more than one or a maximum of two persons at the same time, Costica greets them with a warm welcome and shows them to the tiny kitchen, where everyone somehow found a spot to sit. The family looks tired and hungry. They unpack only one bag with a few clothes, leaving all their other belongings at the door. Silversmith Gypsies used to be travelers. They would roam the country from one corner to another to sell jewelry made by the men. So they are always ready for the road.

Buna hears the noise and heads back inside. She hugs each of her cousins and aunt and asks for their dirty clothes to wash as well. It is April, and it is still cold, so they decide to start the fire on the wood stove. There are only five logs in the kitchen. But the Roma people don't think about tomorrow too much, so they use them all.

"Tomorrow morning, there is a fair nearby," Dinu, Costica's brother, said. "We want to go but are unsure how to get there. Can you and your wife Niculina take us there?"

They decided to leave at dawn together—except for Buna, who had school the next day. Her father might have been the only man to allow his daughter to skip work for school.

In 1970, silversmith Gypsy girls did not go to school. If they did, they abandoned their education around thirteen to fourteen years old. Buna fell in love with the school when she was eight years old, going daily to deliver a meal to her cousin in seventh grade. Every morning she would climb the fence barefoot and watch the kids playing during the break. She did it for more than a year until her cousin convinced his mother to sign her up for the first grade. So, at twenty-one, she was in high school still.

At 6:00 a.m., everybody woke up to start their day. Costica and Niculina were getting their merchandise together while Dinu's family was still waking up. Buna was already up, reading her book under the light of a candle. When everyone got up, she put her schoolbooks aside and attended to her chores. After she finished the laundry and cleaned the house, she served her parents and the guests a meal and wished them well on their journey to the fair.

She shed her long skirt, put on a pair of jeans, took her book bag, and ran out to catch the next bus to the city. Her skin could pass by as being white, so she blended in. No one made any comments when she appeared. She hopped on bus 64 after walking for an hour to get to the first stop.

"Ileana, I was afraid you might be late. Hurry up and take a seat," said the driver.

Outside of her community, she is known as Ileana—the official name.

The bus smelled like a rotten sponge after being used for too long. She took a spot quickly and opened her geography book. She can tell you all the capitals of all the countries in the world. Look at her smile while a love letter falls from the book she is trying to read from. She closes the letter quickly and dives back into her book. The ride is cold, loud, and bumpy, almost to the end, as this part of the city is not paved at all. Her body jumps up and down with the bus, but her eyes are constantly on the book.

After more than one hour, she gets off at Union Square in Baia Mare, where Ana and Claudia—her Romanian best friends—are waiting for her, both looking anxious. They rush to hug each other even before Buna takes the last step out of the bus.

Ana is wearing a white coat and black leather boots, while Claudia is always in some Sergio Tacchini sweatpants and hoody. Buna's jeans look loose, and one can clearly distinguish the various stitches with colored thread, while the sleeves of her black leather jacket are yellow-black, and the zipper is out of service. Her shoes are at least two measures bigger than her feet and have nothing to do with the outfit. The girls head to school together, laughing and cheering. They are ready for the final tests to help them pass from tenth to eleventh grade.

Later that day, she returned home to find more than a dozen men, all sitting around a red carpet, on the floor, discussing. Her uncles, her cousins, and her brothers-in-law were all there. The same number of women were in the kitchen and outside, clearly shaken. All the Gypsies who got injured during the fair were now at her home, and their relatives were as well.

A Romanian man cursed my grandmother for not returning his change fast enough. My grandfather, Costica, demanded an apology. Instead, the man punched him. No one expected them to fight back. Costica and his brother, both Ristina's eldest sons, fought. Soon, the entire fair became a battle between Gypsies against non-Gypsies.

"What happened?" she asked her mother.

"These men got into a fight with some Romanians, and now they are discussing what to do," Niculina replied.

"Are you okay? Why is your eye red?" Buna asked.

"They hit the women as well, as we were trying to cover the bodies of your father and the others," Niculina answered.

"Are they injured? Should anyone go to the hospital?" Buna continued.

"No, they are not so injured, don't worry. Now take these potatoes here and start peeling. We will need a lot of food for everyone," Niculina said while putting some water to boil on the stove.

Costica's left leg was injured already during World War II, and that's why they called him "The Crippled," so the beating took a big toll on him. His inability to defend his family and the humiliation had a bigger impact than the actual pain left in his broken ribs. After talking all day and all night, they decided nothing, and every family left for their own home.

They thought about retaliation many times, and every time, they talked themselves out of it because they were afraid of going to jail. Men in our community may fight each other, but never with the Romanians because they know better. Usually, those who were dark-skinned would go to jail. They had satisfaction knowing the aggressors didn't file a complaint, so there were no police at Costica's home.

"You can't continue school," Niculina told Buna that evening.

"We need you home to take care of your father and to travel with us in the country," Buna's mother added.

That was the day when my mother erased Ileana from her identity, and only Buna was left.

The "good one," mother, that was the day when you accepted your destiny: to continue on the path of silversmith wives, which was not compatible with what Ana and Claudia could have in their lives.

What happened from that moment on until today is your story and mine.

Aunt Matilda (left) & Buna (Mom)

CHAPTER 5

A Square Peg in a Round Hole

When I was five, the smell of freshly made coffee would wake me up in the morning. This was the only moment of the day when our family was alone in our home on Siminocului Street in Bucharest if no relatives were sleeping over, which was often. The three grownups of the household, my parents and grandmother Gutuia, would wake up before sunrise and discuss the day's plans over cups of Turkish coffee. All of us slept in the only heated bedroom during winter, and it shared a wall with the main entrance room, where they enjoyed their peaceful morning before life started.

As my siblings continued their sleep, I would listen in to hear their stories, learn who they were, and where they came from. One cold morning I couldn't hear well, so I decided to pretend I wanted to sleep in my dad's arms, so I crawled out of my covers onto the floor, opened the white door with the broken handle which separated the rooms, and said, "Daddy, I want to sleep next to you, can I?"

The entrance room was always cold, especially during winter, because no one would ever replace the little window missing from our front door. Also, there was a huge space between the door's frame and its bottom, through which snow would make its way inside. The old house had tall ceilings, so any form of improvised heating system would not work well enough. So the three of them were all wearing their coats on their shoulders, and they were also heated by the thick layer of smoke in the room, as each one looked like a chimney with their cigarettes stuck to their lips all the time.

My dad tucked me into his big black coat, and I closed my eyes. They kept talking as if I wasn't there.

"My father never recovered after the war, and that's why he behaved the way he did. You married him knowing what the situation was," I heard my dad saying.

"I did. You are right. He was married with five children, and his wife and youngest son died during deportation, so he returned as someone who had given up on life. But he was my only chance to get married, as you know," his mother said.

"I think you just got desperate," he said lightly.

"You don't know what you are talking about. For a woman not to be married at twenty-five, in those days, was such a shame. If more time had passed, she would have stayed single forever, and you would not have been born," said my mother.

"Yes, he was damaged, much older than her, and an alcoholic. Still, he raised all of you well and was a good father-in-law to me." I heard a sob in my mother's tone.

"I know you only think about his last years, when the beatings got worse and when he truly lost his mind, but overall, he did his best," Gutuia said, while I could hear her taking her cigarette back to her lips from the ashtray.

I only knew my grandfather had died many years before I was born, and he got lost in the last months of his life. I had heard he left somewhere on the streets of Bucharest and never found his way back home. It seemed there was much more to the story than what I knew.

As the sun made its way up in the sky, preparing for the day, my mother took her little suitcase full of accessories to go to the flea market, where she would spend the day selling. She attracted and convinced people in a way that nobody else could. She kissed my forehead, said goodbye to her husband and mother-in-law, and left, barely being able to open the door due to the thick layer of snow and ice covering everything. Son and mother remained pinned to their seats until my siblings woke up, and Grandma had to make breakfast: tea and bread with homemade jam.

In other Gypsy families, men would manufacture the accessories like copper rings or other items, and both the men and the woman would travel the country or other countries to sell those items in fairs or flea markets. His responsibility would be to drive, carry the heavy loads, and make sure they had a place to sleep. Her responsibility was to sell, take care of the children, and ensure food for everyone. For some time, that was the case for my parents, too, before he got too sick to travel or do anything. After, my mom had to buy the accessories and rely on other family members to drive her around the country, or she had to stay in Bucharest and sell at the main flea market.

My father was sick when I met him. My first memory of him involved my mother sticking a needle in his index finger to bring him back to life. Already in his midforties, his heart condition had gotten worse over many years because he refused to obey any rules the doctor imposed. So, he was home most of the time reading or sleeping when we did not have guests. We had an entire library of books, some of which I can't even really understand to this day, such as Goethe or *The Divine Comedy*, which he read multiple times in his life. He would speak to me about them as if I could grasp those complicated words coming out of his mouth, although he would lose me after five minutes. I always fixed my eyes on his words, hoping I could become smart one day and his language would open up for me.

I was always curious how he had been when he was healthy. Once I saw a photo of him and four teenage friends, no shirts on. They had been bathing in a lake close to Alexandria, Teleorman, where he was born. His friends were carrying him on their shoulders, and his smile was wide in this black-and-white photo. The skin on his face was a bit brighter, especially under his eyes. I wouldn't have recognized him if he had not pointed out that he was in the photo. In photos of my mother when she was young, I can clearly distinguish her features, her eyes, and even her hair. He had no resemblance with the young man in the picture, full of life. He finished high school and attended engineering college, from which he could never graduate. Due to his chocolate skin, it was obvious he was a Gypsy, so the discrimination and continuous uphill battle to win a seat at the table wore him down. Outside our community, he was just a dark-skinned boy with big dreams, nothing else but a Gypsy—a second-class citizen and someone unworthy of trust.

"I used to be strong," he told me once, his bold head staring at me.

"Now I am wise." He smiled, almost taking the first sentence back.

He would tell me dozens of stories from his precious books, and now and then, he would confide something precious to me, always in short sentences, so my young brain could capture something of their meaning.

Once, he was reading from *Robin Hood*, the part where he meets the princess, and he stopped to say, "I never regretted marrying your mother. She is the love of my life. You never tell her that, hear me?"

My jaw dropped as I had never heard the word "love" from my parent's mouths. I never told her to this day.

* * *

I was playing with my duck in the main entrance room when we heard heavy steps in the snow. It was already getting late, and it was surprising we hadn't had any visitors by then. Sure enough, six of father's cousins came to visit him. Our house was always full of people, either from my mother's side, as she had two brothers and two sisters, or my father's, as he had three brothers and one sister, each with large families. If it wasn't the immediate family, it was one of the cousins, whom I never stopped to count. I am sure there are over a hundred.

My grandmother served them a bowl of food to taste from it and left the room to allow them to talk. Since I was only five, I was still at the age when I could be around them, so I continued my games with my duck, now in silence, listening in. They had brought a few bottles of liquor, so as soon as the chatter started, the house was stinking of alcohol and food.

"I have plenty! Of course, we can baptize your daughter," said my father, after a few drinks, to one of his distant cousins, whose name I can't remember.

"I will let her know she will be a godmother, and I will dress her and your daughter as princesses," he continued, referring to my mom and the girl he was going to baptize.

Since I was born, I knew we all had to keep my father away from alcohol due to his heart condition. I also knew a girl or a woman should never interfere when men talk, so I kept my thoughts to myself.

"Ah, I am so happy to hear that, my friend," said the distant cousin.

"I am a wealthy man, as you know, so I could have chosen anyone, and still, I wanted you and Buna because you are family people."

I knew his daughter. She was my age and still hadn't been baptized, because they were waiting to throw a party as no one had seen before. I didn't like her because she would brag about her beautiful sandals or beautiful dresses when sometimes I had only one pair of shoes until I outgrew them. I looked at my father, transformed into someone I did not know.

"Let's raise our glasses to the baptism which will soon happen and for the godfather," one of the men said.

I got closer, just to see the commotion. Father barely stood up from his seat, his huge belly in front of him hanging out of his unbuttoned and wrinkled shirt. He cheered and swallowed all the liquor in one shot.

What have I done? is what I read in his eyes.

Mother came back later in the day, and Grandma had made chicken with tomato sauce for all of us. She asked for food the moment she got home. She came into the kitchen, put some sauce on a plate, broke some bread, and dug in as if it were the last meal she would ever have. A few pleasant hours passed, father asleep in the chair he had by the bed, with Dante Alighieri sitting on his lap, Grandma gossiping to my mother, who was not listening, while my sister and I watched TV in the bedroom.

Father woke up and joined the women, so the gossiping stopped.

"How are you?" Father asked Mother.

"My feet are killing me, but I am fine," she said.

I was dreading the moment when he would reveal what he had promised to his cousin.

"He is not telling her," I whispered to Lori. My sister shut me down quickly, bringing her index finger to her closed lips. I knew then that I must stop talking.

"Can you make me coffee?" he said to Mother.

"You can't have another coffee. I can send Rowi to the corner shop for decaf if you really need to have something," responded mother.

"I don't want decaf damn it, I want a real coffee, and besides, I had liquor today with my cousins and your brother, so if that didn't kill me, neither will a coffee," he said, raising his voice.

Caught between his mother and us, she didn't say anything, although she was steaming. I cuddled closer to my sister, hoping to become a fly on the wall.

"Also, I decided we are going to baptize my cousin's girl," he added, now looking at the floor.

Her arms rose to the sky, allowing her palms to fall on her lap with a loud sound.

"What? No, we are not! We barely have food for the family, remember? We can barely pay our bills, so no, we are not baptizing anyone!" she yelled while getting up to make him coffee.

"Yes, we are. We are going to make money and do what I say, you hear?" he said.

"Baby, honey, love," Grandma said, trying to find his eyes. "This woman is working hard, and you cannot afford to spend money on clothing, music, and everything such a party entails," Grandma said.

"Well, I am going to do something and make this happen because I already made a promise," he said.

Grandma lit a new cigarette and brought her long legs underneath her. She knew he couldn't take his word back.

"I know you love your cousins and want to be part of the group, but you are so much better than them. Why do you always try to behave like them? These mistakes you make when you try to act as someone you are not can cost you very much." It was the last thing Grandma said the rest of the night.

Harry (Dad) _ me

Mother returned with the Turkish coffee and poured some
for him, her, and her mother-in-law.

"There you go, now we know you will die faster," she said.

"Buna, I promised my cousin we would baptize his girl," he
said apologetically.

As she was getting ready to start her rant, I ran into her arms and said, "He didn't mean to, mother. I saw it. They made him."

I cried. She looked at me, then at my lost father, and lit a cigarette. No one spoke for what seemed hours.

"I know we can't afford it," father said finally, trying to button his shirt. "So I will take my word back."

"You know you can't. They would shame us for years," mother said.

"People would say our word doesn't mean anything. We have to leave, and you need to help me. So don't drink coffee, go to the doctor, and take your medicines. You will have to drive. We will take the kids to help us carry the heavy load. I cannot protect you forever," she added, looking at the broken window of our main door.

"Yes, we will leave as soon as I go to the doctor, and I have all my medicine with me," he said, studying the floor.

A few weeks later, the two of them, my sister and I, took our merchandise and left for Hungary to sell in a flea market close to the border with Romania. We spent a month there, sleeping in the car, while my mother made enough money for the baptism and for her to start the spring season with a budget for new stock. This was our life on the road.

CHAPTER 6

The Piece of Gum

Gutuia's long black skirt swept the floor as she sat on a stool, smoking a cigarette while cooking at the makeshift stove that matched her 5'9" frame. From time to time, she continued to stir the spoon in the pot while lifting her smoking hand to adjust her head kerchief. Our apartment in Baia Mare was the caretaker of such memories.

My father, her son, was a few inches away from her, sitting cross-legged on a piece of cloth, cleaning some rings made of copper. He liked to spend time with his thoughts, so all you could hear was the sound of the stew cooking in my grandmother's old pot. His hands poured gasoline on a piece of white cloth to gently rub the rust away from the copper rings. Then, with great precision, his long, soft fingers would pass one ring after the other through vinegar to make the shine stay on until the item got to the customer.

Watching his dancing fingers going from brown to purple, to red, and finally black, I always wondered how he could stay put for so many hours when my pet duck and I could not sit still even if we wanted to. During the entire day, his full lips only opened a few times to let us know what we had to do, and his deep hazel eyes could calm my restlessness in a second if I misbehaved. As soon as the lips closed, his eyes would fall back to the dancing fingers that took over him again.

Gutuia, in contrast, yelled at the kids with all the power her lungs could grasp, and although in her late sixties, her eyes were sharp as her black hair. As the steam of the stew engulfed the house, she hovered her nose on top of the pot to smell the ingredients.

"A bit more pepper." She nodded, making the small tumor growing between her eyebrows to shake a bit.

Me, the fly on the wall, I was playing with my duck, making her fly. I realized it was already evening, so one more day had passed. I turned my back to the wall behind me, where my mother drew as many tally marks as the days she would be out. I scratched one more.

Then I wondered what would happen if I screamed loud enough. *Would she be able to hear me all the way in Hungary?*

Because I knew she probably could not hear me, I closed my eyes and imagined myself flying away on top of the city called Miskolc, where she was. I saw her there with her brothers Boi and Ion and her sister Madama. It was a cold evening, so they rushed to put all the merchandise in the cars and find some open taverna to get something to eat.

I imagined it to be one of those days when we could afford to eat a warm meal, and there was joy, as the season was ending and we knew home was closer than ever. I felt satisfied knowing she was safe and would return, as promised.

Meanwhile, in our home, in Baia Mare, two of my mother's cousins cared for me, my sister, and my two older brothers. We all lived together in our one-bedroom, no-restroom apartment in Baia Mare, which was part of a house confiscated from its owners by the communist regime. The entrance, which we called "the yellow room," where my grandma was cooking and dad was working, served as a living room, dining room, kitchen, bedroom for the cousins, and once a week—a bathroom. The two cousins slept here with my grandmother on our only double bed. Most of the time, we had guests—our people traveling through the city, going to different other parts of the country—and they slept on the floor.

There was only one closet for everyone, but I kept my clothes in the pocket of the extendable sofa, where my sister, mother, and I slept until I started going to school. I also snuck my duck into bed when my mother was not home. Otherwise, she had to stay in the yellow room, where it got cold during the night. My sister, Lori, was ten years old and was always out, playing with the other older kids in the shared house where we lived.

There were four families in the complex we lived in, each one with its own apartment consisting of two rooms. We shared the balcony, the front yard, and the latrine.

That week in April was particularly cold, as spring was still fighting a winter that was not giving in, even if she ruined our life entirely for the last six months, making my father sink into days of silence. I had watched over him the night before because he would lose his breath every so often in his sleep. I never knew if he was weeping or if it was because of his heart disease.

Probably his sadness led him to be so silent, cleaning the rings and waiting for his two sons and cousins to come back from selling. My brothers, then young adults, Raymond, nineteen, and Lucian, seventeen, were already breadwinners, so they were expected from their own travels to provide food and money.

After the sunset, Lori appeared first, and Grandma gave her a chore as soon as she opened the door. I took my duck under my arm and jumped from the sofa directly into the other room to hug my sister. Grandma gave us three seconds, arranging her batik once more and raising her left eyebrow to start her ranting about all the things we needed to get done before everyone was back.

"You little brats," she said, raising her hand toward my sister.

"If you don't clean this kitchen up by the time your brothers are back, I will show you," Gutuia said.

Both me and Lori ran to my father's lap.

My father said, "What anger, Mom? Would you calm down? Come on, girls. Do what's needed, and don't upset Grandma."

I left my duck safely on his lap and took a broom to sweep the floor while Lori poured cold water into a pot to warm up for dishwashing.

The food was almost ready, Gutuia made potato stew, and the smell made everyone restless because we knew we couldn't touch it until everyone was back. Father's little finger was twitching from time to time, making my duck wake up for a few seconds just to go back to sleep. I finally reached all four corners of the room, making little patches of garbage to make it easier for me to use the dustpan, and just when I was sweeping the last little patch, Lina (cousin one) came in.

"*Dobroiptumenga* (Hello)," she said in our Romani language.

"*Naistuca* (Hello)," Gutuia and my father responded in one voice.

She kissed Lori's forehead and leaned in to kiss mine, but I crouched right away, seeing steam coming out of her entire being. A short woman, Lina resembled a penguin-monster, with numerous layers under her long leathery jacket, a pair of extra-large gloves, my dad's boots with the top of two pairs of socks coming out of them and a large hat stuck on top of her black batik. She walked heavily toward the bed she shared with the other women to unload all that package off her shoulders. The steam calmed down as layers were coming off, allowing a smell of smoked winter and dust.

My sister's arms were almost entirely in the sink, washing all of Grandma's pots, when Dumana (cousin two) arrived from the other flea market close to us. Both cousins were there selling the jewelry made by my father in different flea markets located near the house. Cousin two also resembled a penguin but had a bit more color, as her batik had a flower imprint, matching her red skirt. Women at that time were not allowed to wear anything but long skirts, no matter the situation.

As she was unloading her heavy clothes, my two brothers opened the door, both of them looking in great spirits.

"Grandma," yelled Raymond, "I missed you."

"What are you saying, boy? I saw you this morning at 4:00 a.m. when you boys left," said Grandma, smiling and hugging my brother's red cheeks.

"My boy," she said, kissing him over and over again.

"Dad, look, we made money today! We sold everything!" said Lucian to our father, who continued to have his gaze pinned to those rings.

"You really did?" he asked while getting up from his seat for the first time that day, putting my sleeping duck aside gently.

"Oh, my boy, we desperately need the money. Show me how much you made?" dad asked.

My older brother took his waist bag and put it in our dad's hands. Dad hugged him for what looked like forever.

"Mother set the table," he said.

Grandma had already taken the only table we had—the folding one—and arranged it properly in the middle of the room. I took the white tablecloth, which always sat on top of our minifridge, and arranged it on the table. My sister brought the two plastic chairs sitting in the corner of the yellow room, and my brothers opened the other three folding chairs hiding under the bed. We sat, and my dad took out all the money from the bag and gave each one of us a pile to count. Although they gave me the smallest pile, I was precise. They had sold all the T-shirts they made that month, so together, we counted one thousand lei, which is how much my mother would bring back after an entire season in Hungary.

The dark skin on my dad's forehead was now chocolate-like again, his eyes forever drawn in, with deep and black circles underneath, all of a sudden magically transformed. My two brothers hugged him, each one from a different side, trapping him between strong hugs to cheer him up. I sighed, watching his eyes getting red and my grandma hiding her tears in her batik, now used as a handkerchief.

The two cousins also gave my father the money they made, no more than fifty lei each. He put it all together and put the money on top of the minifridge.

"We are safe for a few months with this money. Your mother will be so proud of us. Now let's sit down to eat," dad declared.

Grandma placed eight little plates on the table and arranged her little stool closer, while the cousins brought the folding chairs they would carry to the flea markets every day.

My dad served each one of us some stew and bread.

"You added too much onion?" he asks his mother.

"I smell it. It's too strong," dad said.

"First try it, and then we'll decide," Grandma replied, smiling.

He missed my plate, serving me only a piece of bread. He knew I wouldn't eat the stew, as I was picky with food and would, most of the time, prefer to look at it instead of eating it if it was something I didn't like.

He had prepared some rice with milk the other day and kept it for these moments. He served my dish: milk rice and bread. I smiled and thanked him. All of us seated the conversation started:

"Dad, when the guy said he works for a school, I said—so why are you buying for only your two best students?" Lucian said.

"Come on. I will give you a discount if you buy for all thirty-five of them. I saw the way he dressed. He was wealthy, for sure. I gave him a discount, and he bought all of them. I couldn't believe it." My brother's eyes were smiling.

"Yeah, and I went all the way in the other city, in Baia Sprie, to the city center, where I found some people that didn't even speak our language. They were there visiting," Lucian added.

"Why visit? I don't know. But at least they got the best T-shirts in the world, made by Lucian." My brother continued catching his breath.

"Wait, you went so far? You took the train?" asked dad.

"No, I hitchhiked. It's not so far," said Lucian.

"With the heavy bag on your shoulder?" asked dad.

"Yes, a guy took me in his van. It was easy, dad. Don't worry," Lucian concluded.

I was waiting for people to eat parts of their meal so I wouldn't be the first one to finish. My uncles would always make fun of the person who finished their meals faster than everyone else. They even had a name for it: "Hapsan" they called it.

"Nothing moved today, Harry," said Cousin Lina while having her first meal of the day.

"People here know our stuff too well. We need to move out of the city," she said.

"I know. We have to decide when Buna is back," said my dad.

"There is no point in staying here, else we will starve when this money runs out," said cousin two, trying to eat with her swollen fingers sprinkled with blisters.

"For now, we stay, we wait for the others to come back from Hungary, and then we decide," said dad.

"I wish we had bought something sweet to eat tonight to celebrate. We are rich for a week or two, aren't we, dad?" said Lucian.

"I would go buy it for you right now, my boy, but all shops are closed," said dad.

"I found some coins in the market today when I visited Lina, so I bought two gums," I said, taking it out of my pocket to show it to everyone at the table.

I gave one to Raymond to share with Lucian, and I gave my sister the half I kept for her.

"It's cherrylike," I told my brothers, who looked at me surprised.

"The something sweet you asked for," I insisted.

All my siblings, now chewing cherry-flavored gum, ended the day happily. Father was able to breathe throughout the night, and therefore, I did not have to wake up and watch over him.

CHAPTER 7

The Crows Traveling on a Train to Bucharest

The summer of 1994 was making us all miss the long winters of Romania. The sun was melting everyone and everything, the fruits in the main market in Baia Mare were thrown into the garbage at the end of the working day because they would rot if not bought the same day, so we kids would stand in line to get free red melons from the peasants traveling from around Baia Mare to sell their merchandise.

I spent the entire day with my cousin selling rings in the main market while my father went to the city center to finish the authorization paperwork we needed to continue selling in the flea markets.

Veta, my cousin, was sixteen years older than me, so she knew what to do. I was there more to keep her company and count the money. One of the best traders I had ever seen, I loved watching her change her tone of voice and alter her language to fit every person who visited our table. Like a chameleon, she would be warm and polite when an older lady would come up, speaking slowly and patiently, and then she would transform into a mannered, educated, and also tough woman when a well-dressed, tall man would approach us to ask for the price of a ring. The price would always change, depending on the person in front of her, just as my mother had taught her. The same ring was ten lei for the mother and twenty lei for the well-dressed man. It was all in how much she assessed the client could afford or what she considered the client expected the price to be.

"You need to read people, Rowena. You need to know what is in their minds and act accordingly," Veta would remind me every day.

I would nod, intrigued. My mother had taught Veta everything she knew, but she never was able to install that software in my mind. As much as I could read people, I never changed prices to fit the person's clothing, only their expectations.

At the end of the day, we had made three hundred lei, enough to take something home, each of us. I took my money and headed to the end of the market, where I joined the line for melons. They gave me a big one.

"This one is bigger than you, Rowi," the seller shouted, laughing at me, trying to hold the monster in front of my face.

"Thank you, I hope some of it is still good," I replied.

I took the exit closest to that area of the market, crossed the main road, and got to our shared house with a smile up to my ears.

"Oh, it looks delicious," said one of the neighbors, looking down at me from our shared balcony.

"Do you need help with it?" he asked.

"I can make it," I yelled from the back of the melon so that he could hear me.

I climbed the two sets of stairs and finally made it home, where father was waiting for me.

"Rowi, you didn't have to carry this by yourself," dad said.

"It's okay, dad," I said, putting the melon down.

"I know you can't, and I wanted us to have it tonight for dinner," I said.

I left the money Veta and I made on top of the little fridge.

"Will this be enough for us to get the tickets to go to Bucharest to reunite with my siblings?" I asked, trying to make my way to the sink to wash my hands.

"Yes, more than enough. Tomorrow we can go to Bucharest," Dad said.

We would always be traveling between Bucharest and Baia Mare, as the two cities are at the extreme parts of Romania, and from here, we could cover the entire country's fairs.

He cut open the melon, and the smell of sweet candy made my mouth watery. He broke it down into slices and put a few in the fridge. He served two huge slices with white cheese and bread. In the end, both our faces were red and sticky. When we finished, he asked the neighbors to join, and they happily did so. They finished the entire thing. If it were my mom, she would have asked the neighbors to come first, have them eat, and then we would have the leftovers. I have always felt torn about which approach was better.

The next morning, I ran downstairs, crossed the road, and got to my table, where Veta was waiting for me. I told her we would be leaving for Bucharest, and I wouldn't join her for a while. I hugged her and ran back to pack my things. I made my little luggage, packing my one dress, my doll, a few socks, and pants to sleep in during the long train ride. Father also packed a few things in a shopping bag, took his tool bag, and we were off to the train station.

As soon as we arrived, I could see people looking at my father in a different way.

"Fancy people here, dad," I said, trying to smile.

"Yes, baby, very fancy," he answered briefly.

We waited for a while in line to get tickets to Bucharest. The lady at the counter rolled her eyes when she saw us.

"What do you want?" she asked.

"Two tickets to Bucharest, please," father responded quickly.

"Third class for you, mister?" she giggled.

"Actually, couchette, please, I have my daughter with me, and she will probably fall asleep," he said.

"Oh, okay, here it is," she said, her tone now a bit more pleasant than when she started.

We got the tickets and realized we had to run to catch the next train leaving. We got there, running as fast as father could, and found our couchette, number 356, where we would share a tight space with four other people for eleven hours.

We were the first ones in the train compartment. The smell of brown cracked leather and dust was too familiar to both of us. Father opened the stained window to allow air in, took the lowest bed on the left, and placed me on the lowest bed on the right, so he could see me. He knew the moment the train left I would fall asleep. My parents always said I was raised in a car, traveling from one fair to the other, between Romania and Hungary, so I felt comfortable in trains, cars, or buses. I fell asleep as soon as the train whistled for departure, allowing the soothing sound of its wheels to ease me into dreamland.

I woke up sometime later. There were other people now in the couchette, but dad was not there. I put my slippers on and went outside to find him. He was right at the door of the couchette, watching the landscape pass in the windows. He took my hand and continued chasing the river Bistrita accompanying us. We were both mesmerized by the beauty of the colors when I heard a loud voice shouting, "Crows are not allowed on trains!"

I turned my head to see a tall man, maybe in his fifties, surrounded by other men similar to him, that were standing down the hallway of the train, repeating loudly, "Crows are now allowed on trains."

I looked at my father, who was still gazing at the landscape.

"What is he talking about, dad? Where can he see crows on the train?" I asked my father.

"Never mind him, baby," he said to me.

I was dying of curiosity and could not ignore his loud comments.

"You will never be part of us. You should know your place. You disgust us."

Father's eyes were now red and still fixed on the window.

"Dad, where are the crows?" I asked again.

He turned me to face him, and he turned his back on the group of people in the hallway.

He looked at me, eyes red and trembling low lip. "It's us, baby, and unfortunately, you have to know this. Some people don't like us because we are Gypsies. They don't know us. They just believe they do," dad said.

I nodded, confused.

He took me back inside the couchette. Everyone else was sleeping, so he put me on his bed. He sat close to me and whispered, "You will start school next year, and you will be more in their world, so you might hear people talking badly about you because you are Gypsy. But you always have to know what's in your heart. Never let them get to you," my dad said.

"Do they ever get to you, dad?" I asked.

"Too much, too many times, but I know you are stronger than me," he said.

I closed my eyes and waited for him to lie down in his bed. As soon as I heard his breath sinking into sleep, I opened my eyes and made him a promise in a whisper. "I will never be afraid of anyone. For you."

PART TWO

GROWING UP
ONE AFTERNOON

CHAPTER 8

Silence and Howls

The cruel smell of the blue corridors of Vitan hospital woke me up. I was dragging my feet behind my mother for the last thirty minutes, walking here. She got me out of bed at 6:00 a.m. that September day in 1998 because we had an appointment at the doctor. The pediatrician of all the kids in my community was going to read my blood tests.

As soon as we entered, there were three glass rooms on the right, each one with a label: Rubeola, Measles, and Mumps. Five women were waiting with their children in front of the doctor's door. The smell of medicine and alcohol mixed with cheap detergent. We all knew the drill. You needed to bathe the night before you went to the doctor. If we showed up the way we were when we played on the brownfields in our neighborhoods, the doctor would scold our mothers.

I hated the big clock on the wall because his minutes did not go by as fast as other clocks. Time was not in a rush on these corridors, as there was nothing to do other than wait. But that morning, I found something to distract myself:

study the skin on my mother's neck. Silky and magical; there was enough skin to gather between my fingers, pinch for a second and then drop. I caressed each wrinkle one by one and counted them up and down as she was speaking to the other women.

"Rowi, I am speaking to the lady. Go play," she said when I pinched a bit too hard.

I continued caressing and sometimes even kissing the little dark spots.

Finally, after some time, the assistant called us in. She took my weight and height and sent me in with my mom.

"How does it all look, doctor?" mother asked.

"She is healthy, Buna." the doctor quickly responded.

"But you do need to be careful with her heart, as you know she is at risk for rheumatic heart disease," she added.

She looked at me, she looked at the doctor, and said, "But she doesn't have it now, right?"

"No, but it might start later," the doctor concluded.

"I understand, but now we are good," mother said and got up to leave.

We left in a hurry, and she dragged me again, now to the tram station close to home.

"Okay, now go home and take care of your father," she said, waiting for the tram to take her to the flea market.

"Yes, Mom, but I have school later," I said.

"Your brother will come to take him to the doctor by then," she said.

The tram arrived and she left. I crossed the road and headed home. Just before turning the last corner to arrive, I met my cousin, Ramona, who was at the shop buying bread. Ramona lived ten minutes away from my place.

"Hey, you want to come to play at my house until school starts?" she asked.

"I can't," I said. "I need to stay with my dad, and I don't think he will allow me."

"You wanna go ask him?" she said.

"Yes, let's go ask him," I said.

The sun was now fully shining, and the little Siminocului Street was blazing with children and people walking up and down. Ramona and I opened my old gate in complete silence, not to bother my father, who was either watching TV or reading.

"I will wait for you right here," Ramona said, whispering, as soon as we entered the gate.

"All right, I will be back to tell you if I can go or not," I said in a low voice.

I took a few more steps to get to the door, silently entered the living room, and opened the door slowly to where he was. The TV was on, and he was snoring.

"Hey, dad, it's me, Rowi," I said, touching his hand gently.

"What, what?" he said, waking up scared.

"Dad, are you okay?" I said.

"Yes, I am. What is it?" he replied.

"Do you need me? If you don't, I want to go play at Ramona's place," I said.

"Yeah, go and play there," he said, laying his head back down on the chair and closing his eyes.

I paced myself back the same way I came in. I ran on my tippy toes to the gate.

"He said I can go," I told Ramona.

We both hugged and opened the gate, touching it as if it was an egg about to break.

We giggled and ran all the way to her home, where her siblings Sergiu and Delia were already playing hide-and-go-seek indoors. They were two years younger than Ramona and one year younger than me. Together, we were an inseparable team. Home alone, we could do anything we wanted until noon because school started at 1:00 p.m., and it was ten minutes away from us.

"I am the warrior king," Sergiu announced in the living room, pounding his chest and making the sound of a lion.

"Meah, you are a weak monkey," his older sister replied.

"I am Mowgli, the jungle boy," she continued, climbing on top of the sofa.

"And who am I?" asked Deli.

"I am Baloo, and you are Bagheera," I decided, squeezing her short frame in my long arms.

"We're your friend, we're your friends, we're your friends to the bitter end," we all sang in one dramatic voice, the song we had heard so many times while watching and rewatching *The Jungle Book*.

Each one of us started shaking our bodies, getting ready to chase each other back and forth in the house and then outside, in the tiny yard, to copy what the animals would do every time there was a singing moment in the movie.

"It's almost time," I said, looking at the big clock on their living room wall after catching my breath from the last run.

"All right, but we continue tomorrow morning?" Sergiu asked.

"We'll see," I said, tying my shoes to return home for my bookbag.

"What are you doing here?" said Anghelina, their mother, walking in, crying, looking at me as if I killed someone.

"You know you should take care of your father. Why are you here playing? This is your fault. He is dying! Go now, go home!" she shouted with all her might.

Her children ran away to their room.

"Dad said I could come," I cried and froze.

"Go home, I said!" she shouted once more and picked up the home phone. I ran away.

I once heard almost fifty thousand people die of stroke each year in Romania. In a country of only nineteen million people, the numbered is considered high.

Let's say I knew all of this when I found him.

Let's say that at ten years old, I could discern my emotions, and with calmness and eloquence, I was to tell you the story of this person, my father—like a reporter would, objectively.

From what I can tell, he had fallen from the chair, an old, gray upholstered chair. I could see the yellow rubber sticking out from the arms, all the way from where the hands would rest to the ground. It's mid-September and sunny, so even if the lights were not on in the room, I could see him gasping for air with his eyes rolled back. He was saying something, but I could not hear.

I ran here, so I was also gasping. My heavy legs fell, making a sharp noise.

My eyes fell on the dusty carpet. The dark velvet and green flowers were fading. His fingers were touching the fringes. The walls were covered with a decorative rug portraying *The Abduction from the Palace.* There were many photos on the wall facing the large windows. One of them had his name on it. I estimated it was a black-and-white portrait of a young man in his late twenties. His eyes were big and dark. He was smiling in a way that made me straighten my back, raise my chin, and even smile back. The fallen person had no resemblance to the portrait. I checked to see, but nothing was there. Books scattered across the room; some opened on different pages, a few on the floor, one close to the chair, one on the chair. He was reading when he died.

So, what can we interpret about my father? What did I know about my father, really?

He was tall.

He was too dark-skinned to be a Romanian.

He read too much for his Gypsy cousins.

He was tired all the time.

He smoked two packets of cigarettes every day.

He asked to eat everything I ate, which was sweet.

He read Goethe, Sartre, Dickens, Herman Melville, and Proust was his favorite.

He did not like people too much, especially when he was sick and tired.

He was sick and tired often.

I was one of his caregivers.

My mother liked him sometimes.

Death is a common thing, but seeing death happen at ten years old destroys. It cuts off the world for many years, or better said, it transforms the world into a sarcophagus. When you see your father in his last moments fallen on the ground, lost, his image will forever be of a man struggling to die. But who was he beyond all of this? Did he really want to live?

I fell to my knees.

"Come back, please. Don't leave me alone. Take me with you," I whispered gently to his ear, wiping the white bubbles from the corner of his mouth.

I took his hand in mine and begged him with all my heart not to leave me alone, just as I did so many times when he would lose his breath during the night. He would come back every time, so I was hopeful and decided to lie down next to him to give him my warmth. I am still waiting in my dreams, twenty-five years later.

I was still lying close to him when two strong arms lifted my body.

"Go away, go away!" my brother Lucian said, handing me off to our neighbor.

As the woman next door tried to comfort me, I heard my cousin Carmen screaming at the gate.

"The ambulance, bring the ambulance!" she was saying.

I ran outside and saw my father lying on the pavement. My brother and Carmen drug him outside and were waiting for the ambulance. It took more than thirty minutes for a huge truck with no equipment but only a tiny sign in front saying *"Ambulance"* to get there. The doctor and the assistant needed two other people to lift my father's body to the back of the truck.

I watched them leave and kept repeating: "I know you can hear me, don't leave me alone."

My brother took me in his car, and we drove to the hospital. As soon as we got to the courtyard entrance, we heard our mother's screams and then a wild noise like a building collapsing. Both of us ran to the emergency room.

A doctor was waiting for us in front. "Are you with Mr. Marin?" he asked.

"We are his children," Lucian said.

"I am so sorry," he said and directed us to another white door, not the ER.

We stepped into a full room. His brothers, his sister, his cousins, and my mother surrounded my father. My mother's hair was on the floor next to her in huge strains, and she was bleeding from her hand. I looked up and saw the only window in the room shattered and full of blood also.

"This is your fault. You killed him," she said to my brother and me.

I have no remembrance of what my brother said or did, but I know I hugged her, and she didn't throw me away. She just continued sobbing and crying, and so did I.

I never again touched the skin of her neck, and I never played *The Jungle Book* again with my friends.

CHAPTER 9

The Good Daughter

"You can be such a disappointment." I heard the voice of one of my father's older nieces saying when I looked at the seat where she sat every time she visited.

She never actually used those words, but that's what I thought her eyes would say during every ceremony we held for my father's death. In the Romanian Orthodox Church, during the first year of mourning, we hold a commemorative ceremony almost every month and after the first year, once a year up until year seven. Our family extended that period to more than fifteen years. But during the first year, we held each and every ceremony with more than one hundred people, all extended family. This allowed plenty of time for my community to show or tell me what I should do and how I should behave to be a good daughter to my mother.

Me, I spent the afternoon eating chocolate wafers. I was twelve and was supposed to clean the house for Christmas time. Mother was gone for a few days to sell merchandise in a flea market close to Bucharest. I was supposed to clean the carpets, wash the windows and the floors, and handwash the dirty laundry. In fact, I'd boiled the water on the stove twice, and classified four piles of clothing based on color to make it easier for me so that I wouldn't have to change the water in the basin every time it would get black or red. I was just about to start with the white shirts when that voice of craving would start again. The sweet bitterness of dark chocolate from the last piece would tickle my taste buds, and the voice would scream again for more. I decided it would be the last one, and then I could finish the laundry and all the chores my mom left me with. I rolled up my sleeves and started reheating the water for the third time.

I decided to hide the bag of wafers away from me, so I took it and extended my arm as far as I could in order to leave it on the highest shelf in the kitchen.

"That's that!" I said.

"No more! I am going to finish and make my mom proud," I said to nobody.

I heard my best friend. I ran outside to open the gate. I was surprised. No one was out, and I must have imagined it. Yesterday's blizzard left a lot of snow and ice, so not a soul would even want to breathe this cold air. They say its dryness and low temperature can instantly cause lung problems.

I went back inside to continue my long list of chores. I'd been doing such a good job since I was six or seven years old. Why was I dragging my feet now? I slammed the kitchen door, trying to get back to where I had left the water boiling. The shabby furniture shook for a second, enough to make the bag of waffles fall from the shelf and back on the counter.

My heart raced. I felt water in my mouth, my taste buds screaming at me, and I saw my hand opening up the bag without my consent.

I wished I could go back to when I was doing such a good job, with ease and without distraction. Anything to make my mother's life easier and continue earning my badge of "little helper." Like homework: even if it's difficult, sometimes not necessary, or even unfair—I had to do it. If not, I would have to confront my mother's ugly side, which appeared from time to time, summoned by people around her that don't do everything she says when she says it. If my hat of "the little helper" was taken away from me, I would be nothing; unworthy. I wanted to keep my hat. I longed for my life to remain as it was, where I knew the rules, and I followed them by the letter. But now, more and more frequently, I found so many obstacles: my group of friends, my mirror showing parts of me stretching in ways I hated, my older sister's makeup, and my cravings. So many cravings! But the chocolate wafers were the ones I couldn't set aside until I finished the bag.

By the time the water was boiling for the third time, I had a waffle in my right hand and a magazine in another one. I was reading something about a celebrity that wore a tight red dress at a fancy party while bloated. I couldn't tell she was, I thought, while the salty caramel made its way from the tip of my tongue to the cheek, under the tongue, tossing and turning, finding new ways to thrill me. I was enjoying each inch of each waffle slowly, as if it were the last one on the planet. The sound of the boiling water was what woke me up. I decided I would wash and eat, so I finally poured the water into the basin, ready to start. I placed the first white items inside, added the detergent, and immediately heard the craving voice: one more, the last one. I need to let the water cool off, so why not, I said. Half an hour later, I had almost finished the bag and the magazine.

What happened to me? The chocolate wafers were controlling me. Discipline, obedience, my entire identity—all gone. My mind, my eyes, and my hands were not mine. They kept taking me back to that damned bag, even if I told them not to. I was afraid that whatever my mom would tell me to do, I would not be able to achieve, as an invisible force led me to act as a different person, not myself, the self that I know.

What saved me was looking at that seat again, now intentionally. I wanted to hear the voice in my ears telling me how worthless I was and "such a disappointment." I allowed myself to bathe in that feeling until my disobedient voice calmed down and almost disappeared. It was dark outside when I finished the laundry and the floors. I had rolled every carpet in the house to take outside to wash, scrubbed the wooden floors with detergent, hung all the laundry by the clothing line in our yard, and was getting ready for the worst part—opening the windows for the cleaning when my sister came by.

My sister, Loredana, left home two years before my father died. Although my sister, my parents adopted her from her real father (my mother's brother) when she was still a baby because her birth mother died. So now, Lori was living with her real father in a rented apartment, together with two family members on her father's side, both drug addicts. Mother made my sister leave because a boy from our community that lived nearby liked her, and his mother did not agree with this. So, to stop anything that could happen, although they were both fourteen years old, she kicked Lori out. That's how important the reputation of a girl and a family were. Nothing was more important than keeping the name of the family clean.

I didn't see Lori for the first year, which broke my heart and hers. But then, when I couldn't bear it anymore, I took an older cousin and visited my sister at the "drug addict's home." That's how, two years later, she and I were sisters again, just living in different houses.

"What are you doing?" she said, seeing me on top of a cabinet, trying to reach the top part of the windows.

She was visiting to make sure I was okay.

"Are you crazy? It's freezing outside. Close those damn windows."

"Hey, Lori, I jumped down from the cabinet to hug her."

"Finally, someone that loves me," I told myself.

"It's okay. I will just clean them a little bit. I need to finish because Mom is coming back tomorrow, and everything must be ready. How are you? Do you need anything?" I said, trying to climb back on the cabinet.

She gave me a long, stern look, but she knew what I felt.

"Okay, give me a piece of cloth and some of that alcohol for the windows. If we both do it, we can get this done in a few hours," she said.

She climbed on another cabinet and started whipping the other windows.

"I came here to tell you I got a job at a factory. I am going to clean bottles a few hours a day and make some money for my father and me," she said.

"A factory? You don't want to sell at the flea markets like everyone else does?" I asked, while trying to clean a stain.

"I can't. I have no one to help me do that," she said.

Both of us were silent for a long time, finishing up the chores and keeping each other company.

We finished everything very late, so she stayed and slept with me. I cuddled in her arms the entire night, stealing her warmth, just like we used to do when we were kids. Her long body and big feet made the perfect nest to sleep all night uninterrupted. I didn't hear any of the night noises that usually would keep me up frightened. I felt safe. We woke up on December 23 with the house clean and ready to receive the massive number of people we knew will come to visit my mother that year to remember my father. It was clean and warm, and we knew there would be food when she arrived.

We heard my uncle Udila's car around 10:00 a.m. The car was full of luggage and food. My sister and I put on our jackets and ran outside to help mother unload.

"It's clean," she said after we put away everything, and she finally sat down on the chair my father's niece would sit.

"My sister helped me, Mom. Otherwise, I would still be cleaning," I said, looking at my shoes.

"Of course, you would have," she added.

"Now, go open those bags because there is fish there. Clean all of it. We need to start cooking."

I looked at Lori, hoping she understood this was a good time for her to leave and avoid the tremendous workload ahead. She shook her head in disagreement and took those bags of fish herself. We continued working together the entire day, allowing mother time to rest.

Although the relationship between her and Mom was not great, since Father died, my sister put her resentment away to be there for me. During those times of mourning my father, the only person in my family next to whom I could find comfort, was my sister, as she understood me best, although we never spoke of feelings. She was there, like a rock to grab onto when the heavy waters of grief continued to surround my family. I would come back to her, or she would come back to me whenever we needed fuel to go on our paths. As much as I was a disappointment to people around me, I knew I'd never be anything less but worthy of love in my sister's eyes.

CHAPTER 10

Admission for Gypsies

You don't allow a customer to leave the table until you sell something! This was my mother's motto I had to live by.

"You won't find anything like what I've got, mister. My merchandise is unique and brings good luck. You will find fortune when you wear this ring because you got it from me," I shouted in a man's face as I competed with the ear-splitting sounds of music coming from the Ferris wheel, bumper cars, and roller coasters.

Călărași is a small city in Romania, close to the border with Bulgaria, and our place to go every year in May, during the city's yearly fair, to sell our fake jewelry. The year 2001 was special because I was preparing to take the end-of-middle-school exam, which would hopefully get me into high school.

I worked hard those three days to be as convincing as possible, sell as much as I could, and get time to study in the evenings.

Some people smiled politely and left, while others fell for it. Even if I was only thirteen, I looked seventeen at least, due to my height, so some men would flirt with me. When there was room for convincing through flirting, I did it, regardless of the dirt under their nails, while I helped them try on rings. The Călărași fair was fruitful, and by the end of the day, when the other silversmith women made their rounds, bragging about how much money they made, my mom and I giggled because we had made more than anyone else.

The train was leaving at 5:00 a.m., so we slept at the fair, with me in my cousin's car and her with other older women in her nephew's car. The men slept outside, watching the merchandise and the cars filled with women and children, most of whom were not theirs. I spent the night glued to the window, on the back seat, with two older cousins, trying to read using the light coming from the Ferris wheel. On the second day, I had a simulation for the final exams, and I wanted to get the best results I could get. At dawn, my mother came with one of her cousins to wake me up.

"Come on, your uncle is going to take us to the train station," she said.

An uncle, cousin, nephew, niece, or something, would always come through to help mother and me get by.

I hopped on; happy we didn't need to take a bus to the train. One hour later, we arrived at Bucharest Central Train Station, where one of my two brothers, Lucian, was waiting for us. He is thirteen years older than me and two years younger than Raymond—our eldest brother. He took us to his apartment, where we could take a good shower. Back at my home, we still didn't have warm running water, so showers meant boiling water in big tanks and pouring it from the tanks onto our bodies. So from time to time, we would either use the shower at my brother's place or the one in neighboring big buildings with central heating stations. After the shower, my brother drove me to school for the exam simulation.

The tests were painfully hard, and the wait for the results was worse. Even my Romanian literature teacher—the only one who believed in me —was nervous. After a week, all eighth graders rushed to see our names on a white piece of paper glued to the main entrance of the school building. I was heartbroken to see a seven out of ten. I wouldn't get into any of the best high schools in Bucharest without a score above 9.50 minimum.

"Oh, you will be fine. The important thing is going to high school. It doesn't matter which one," mother said on the day of the results.

She never stepped foot in my school building. The only contact person my teachers had was my older brother Raymond. So, she had no idea the expectations my teacher had of me, the only Romani girl in the school to attend an Olympic championship at a national level. A seven was absolutely not acceptable. I was afraid of facing my teachers more than anything else.

One morning I built up the courage and said, "I can't go to the fairs anymore. Not until I finish all the actual exams in two weeks. "Please, can I stay home and study?" I pleaded.

"Okay, stay. I will manage," she said while cutting a piece of meat into two and tossing it in the boiling water to make a soup.

I opened my Romanian, math, biology, and geography books—all the exam books I needed. I was going to read all of them again in these weeks. To dedicate sixteen to eighteen hours a day to studying, someone else had to cover for me with the chores around the house, and of course, my sister was my rescue. Now that she moved in with us after I almost begged her to forgive mother and return, she could take on my responsibilities for a week, even though she still worked every day, now as a waitress at a gas station.

I did not do anything else but study at the little white table in the bedroom I shared with my mother and sister. I only moved away to go to the bathroom and sleep at the end of the day. After eight days, I finished reading all four books again. I spent the rest of the time doing math problems and trying to understand if I got it right or not by asking whoever came to visit and had some idea. One of my mother's nephews was particularly good at math, although he abandoned school in the ninth grade because he married. He would spend hours with me trying to figure out geometry problems that seemed impossible to understand.

The tests started beginning of June, two every week. The first one was Romanian literature, the only one I was hoping to have under control because I had participated a few times in Olympics for storytelling. Despite this, the moment they sat us down and gave us the subject, my heart collapsed in my stomach. I imagined myself as part of a story I wrote a year before about a giraffe who shrunk over time as she, too, wanted to become invisible.

Nothing made sense, my vision was blurry, and my breathing was quick and shallow. I took a sip of water and decided I was only going to tackle the first question in the exam, not the whole thing.

The room was completely silent, so my mind would jump around to people's pencils on the paper or to the supervisor's dress that was making a fine and elegant sound every time she walked around to check on us. I closed my eyes and imagined myself as invisible and able to leave the room and go outside to breathe air. I inhaled a few times deeply and opened my eyes again to my empty piece of paper. More than thirty minutes had passed, and I had nothing, but for the first time, the letters in the questions looked familiar.

I answered the first question, and from there, the information just poured onto the paper from some source unknown to me. I was almost the witness of my hand, writing with grace and confidence. I was among the first to turn in my papers. From there, the other three exams seemed more manageable and even exciting.

The morning the results arrived, I couldn't move from the bed. I had nausea and was shivering throughout the night. Mother helped me dress, for the first time in many years, because I could barely put my pants and shirt on. She prepared water with lemon and gave me a calcium pill to calm my nerves. A cousin of hers appeared. She was visiting on her way to the flea market. When she saw me in such bad shape and my mother not knowing what to do with me, she decided to go to the school with us. She slipped her arm under my waist and half-carried me while my mother was trying to encourage me. When we almost got there, a woman came out of her yard to toss a bucket of water on the street. Both mother and her cousin almost jumped up, thrilled.

"This means luck! Water means luck before such moments! You've done great. We know it!" they both shouted in my ears.

My jaw and my fists finally unclenched, and I was able to swallow the feeling of bursting into tears.

My Romanian teacher greeted me in front of the main door, with tears in her eyes, hugging my mother and me.

"You made it, girlie. You made it! Go see!" my teacher said.

I climbed the ten stairs to the main door, where they had glued white papers to the windows. I had one of the highest scores, more than any of my Romani cousins attending the same school. I was ecstatic for days. I could not believe I made it.

The next week, we found out which high schools had admitted us based on our grades. My goal was to get into one of the top five in the city. I only made it in the top ten, which was not what I aimed for.

My teacher saw the disappointment in my eyes and said, "You know you can always choose to declare you are a Roma, which would allow the system to use the Roma-dedicated spots that each high school has."

I was shocked to hear I could benefit from the fact I am a Roma when normally one could only expect the worst from declaring to belong to my ethnicity.

"No, I did not know," I said. "Let me see what my mother says about this."

"So, I got into a good high school, but it's not one of the best in the city, so I could move to the one I want if I declare I am a Roma," I brought this up with my mother after she came back from the flea market.

"What do you mean? Why would you want to declare yourself a Gypsy officially? Do you know your uncles and aunts were deported to Transnistria because the government knew they were Gypsies? What if another war comes? They will take us all because you wanted to get into the best high school?" she said, eyes wide open, clutching her fists on her legs.

"I didn't think of it this way," I said honestly. "Do you think it is a real danger?" I asked.

She sighed and looked away, saying, "Let's ask your brothers. They will know what to do," she decided.

She went to the bedroom, picked up the home phone, and dialed Raymond's number.

"Come home tonight and bring your brother," she said.

A few hours later, the living room was full. My sister was home, and both my brothers came with their wives.

"This girl wants to declare us Gypsies officially. Should she do it?" mother asked, looking at Lucian.

"What's the occasion?" Raymond asked jokingly.

"I got into Elena Cuza when I wanted to go to Șincai because it's one of the best high schools. I can't get in unless I try to get into one of the places dedicated to Gypsies. This means signing an official document declaring our ethnicity," I tried to explain myself.

"Oh really, you got in? Congrats!" said my brothers as they gave me a hug.

"Mom, this is not communism anymore, we won't get deported, and they won't make us slaves ever again. It's safe now, don't worry." Raymond said, relaxing his back on the sofa.

"Also, if they want to deport us, you think they don't already know we are Gypsies? They do, believe me," Lucian added.

I could see how this last piece really convinced her.

"Yes, they probably do. All right, tomorrow go declare and move to Șincai. It's better because it's much closer than the other one so that you will be home sooner," mother decided.

I finally got into one of the top high schools in Bucharest, where there were only two of our kind: myself and a cousin whose mother insisted she would go wherever I would go. That autumn began the four toughest school years of my life, as I tried my best not to be a Roma student but just a student like everybody else.

CHAPTER 11

The Dragon

In 2005, the holiday season started at 5:00 a.m. on December 6 with a trip to The Dragon, a wholesale store on the outskirts of Bucharest which supplied the city with items from China. My mother and I bought the right to sell in Bucharest's second-most central plaza. We had twenty-one square feet and less than three weeks to recover our investment in the merchandise and make profits to ensure our Christmas groceries.

Every year, as the holiday lights turned on in the country's major cities, Romanians occupied their mind and time with carols and hunting gifts. The silversmith community was there to serve them every time, selling seasonal items from before sunrise to after sunset, on the streets, from the beginning of the month up to the evening when Jesus was born. On this night, the Romani women could afford to start preparing their household for Christmas.

"Come on, Rowi. It's time," I heard my mother say in my dream.

She opened the door to my room completely, came closer to my bed, and said, "Are you awake? Come on. It's getting late."

I opened my eyes and saw her frame against the large window. It was still dark outside, and the only thing I could hear from the street was the noise of the wind moving the snow. She was already dressed, I realized.

"Are you ready?" I asked, trying to open my glued eyes.

"Yes, I am ready. The Dragon is already open, and we need to get there before everybody else. Otherwise, we will miss out on the good merchandise, so hurry up!" she said, walking away.

I woke up and sat on the bed for a few more minutes as I remembered what was happening. It was Saint Nicholas Day—my father's name day and one of those days in the year when we were poor. I sighed and put on two pairs of pants, two pairs of socks, and two sweaters on top of an undershirt. I put on my winter boots and the winter jacket I got from my sister-in-law. Mother finished her cigarette, put on her jacket, and we left. We walked and took a bus, a tram, and a shuttle to get to the Dragon.

"How much is this?" my mother asked a merchant, showing him a pack of scarves.

"No for you," answered the merchant in bad Romanian.

"I take many. How much per pack?" mother adapted her Romanian to his bad one.

"Five lei," he finally answered, inviting her to leave, with his hand.

She turned to me and said, "Nobody has these in the plaza where we sell. This guy only sells to people who buy in bulk. What can we do to buy a few to test them out?"

I raised my chin, grew a few inches taller, took the pack from my mother's hands, and placed myself so close to this man's face that I could smell his breath.

"You think we can't buy many because you see my mother is old? You filthy person with no respect for elderly people. I can buy your entire store if I want to, and I wanted to maybe do business with you long term because your merchandise is good. You don't deserve it. You deserve not to sell anything and to go back home empty-handed today," I said, throwing a pack of scarves on top of his merchandise and turning my back on him.

"Let's go, Mom. We are not doing business with him," I said, walking away.

My mother was annoyed. "What are you doing?" she whispered as I took her arm to leave.

"Let's see if it worked," I said.

We walked out of his shop, and a kid came to us just before we turned the first corner.

"Ma'am, come back. The boss wants to sell to you," he said.

I smiled and walked back. We only got ten packs; just what mother intended. I told *the boss* that now we were offended.

We would buy only a small number of packs to test his merchandise. But if the test proved successful, we would buy thirty dozen next time.

We left before 6:30 a.m., with two big bags of merchandise, to the plaza where we were going to sell. The shuttle was extremely crowded. There were no seats, so we had to stand for forty minutes while holding our bags closely. Mother was always scared of people trying to steal from us. We had to fight for a seat on the tram, and finally, the bus was better. We arrived at our table in the plaza at 7:30 a.m., and I was happy to see two of my cousins already there unpacking.

"You are here!" Casi yelled at me with her high pitch and great energy.

"Let's finish and get some warm tea," I said, hugging her.

We both returned to our tables, aligned on the same row. We were more than twenty families, and therefore, we made a row of twenty tables, every twenty-one square meters, with only a tight space between them.

The place you got in the row was extremely important. You didn't want to have your table at the beginning because clients would rarely stop there, and you did not want it at the end because the clients would have already bought something by the time they got to you.

Both my cousins and I had our tables close to the end because we didn't have the right connections at the mayor's office. I was confident because my mother always assured me: *"each one of us has our own luck."* I kept on telling myself this motto as I was unpacking our merchandise from The Dragon, displaying it as nicely as possible on our table. After about an hour, we were ready to receive clients.

"Good morning, beautiful Madam. How may I help you today?" Mom said to the first person who stopped at our table.

I knew this was her jam, so for now, it was safe to leave her alone.

"Going to get tea and will be back," I said while she was wiping the snow from the pack of scarves to show the lady the colors.

"Hello, Auntie, may this day be fruitful," I greeted Casi's mother.

"Good day Rowi. How is your mother?" asked my aunt, barely breathing under her massive winter coat.

"Attending clients, so doing well," I said.

She chuckled, "Nobody does it better than her," she said, nodding.

"Good morning, Uncle," I greeted Casi's father. They created what looked like a small tent for him to sit down on a chair and be protected. Normally men stay at home or in their cars while women sell, so I was surprised to see him there.

"Hello, Rowena. Good day," he said with his deep voice, looking away.

"Casi, I am going to get some tea. Can you come?" I asked.

"Mom, are you okay here?" she asked, shivering, her lips purple and her cheeks red.

"Yes, go. Don't stay too long," Casandra's mom said.

The café was just a few meters away from our table. As soon as we got in, everybody turned to stare at us. People were nicely dressed, enjoying a coffee or a sandwich, while Casi and I looked like Eskimos. We covered every inch of our bodies with three layers of clothing, and both of us were wearing thick hats and our jacket hoodies on top. We ignored the looks and took off the hoodies and the double gloves to ask for tea.

"Oh, you poor things, you sell outside?" an elder lady asked at the counter.

"Don't worry, ma'am. This is what we do. We are used to it. We have thick skin," Casi answered in a dismissive tone.

"Yes, we do," I answered more politely. "We have good jackets, so don't worry about us," I took the teas and sat down at the counter with Casi.

"Aren't you going to school anymore?" she asked.

"Definitely not today. I can't leave mother alone, and I don't have time to go change. But some days I do need to go because we have exams in a week," I said.

"Yeah, I am definitely not going. I can't. We will never be like them. I am telling you, no matter how much I know you want it," she said, looking around at the others.

"I don't know anything anymore, Casi. Maybe you are right. I don't know. What are you gonna get for the wedding after Christmas?" I asked, trying to change the subject.

"Oh, depending on how this season will go, I want to buy a beautiful dress because Remus will be there. And you?" she asked.

"I need a new pair of shoes," I said.

"Yes, we will get dresses and shoes and everything we need. Just wait and see," she was trying to say when one of our older cousins came to the table.

"So you left to get tea and forgot about your mothers, huh?" she said.

"We sat down ten minutes ago," I said apologetically.

"Well, go, now. They are both waiting for you," our cousin said.

We put back our hats, hoodies, and gloves and ran back to take our places. It was true. Both our mothers were waiting for us because this was the rush hour: between 8:30 a.m. and 9:30 a.m., so it was crucial to make the most out of it.

The first half of the first day was productive, we sold most of the scarves at high prices and were also successful with our undershirts.

The afternoon was slower, so I sent my mother out for food.

"Mom, go indoors to warm yourself a bit," I said.

"I am fine," she said, lighting a new cigarette.

"Okay, then go to the supermarket and get us some food," I said.

She agreed and left for the nearby supermarket.

I was attending to a lost client, showing him a leather wallet, when I saw my high school classmates Diana and Cristina sitting behind my table, watching me and giggling.

"Thank you, Sir, have a great day! I will be waiting for you to come back with your wife to get more gifts for the family," I told my client, trying to keep a straight face.

"What are you two doing here? Aren't you supposed to still be in school? We have a geography class right now," I said, laughing and hugging them.

"Oh, don't worry, our teacher will not miss any of us," Diana said. "We came to see you. We were worried about you, and we brought you this thermos with warm tea."

"As you said, it's freezing, and you are the one sitting here all day," Cristina said.

"I am okay, don't worry. This is what we do. My people and I have thick skin," I said.

"Oh, you don't have to hide from us. We are here for you. Look, I can even sell if you want me to. I can sell while you attend one or two classes per day," Diana said.

"You wouldn't last in this cold for two hours, Di, and besides, I am not sure about your selling skills, I must say," I said.

You could hear our laughter from across the street.

"Look, you have to come to school next week, really. We have those exams, and also, we are a team. We need you with us," said Cristina, pulling her sweater sleeves onto her hands, shivering.

"She will," mother said, returning with a bag of food. "I just needed her for these first days and last days, but next week she will come to school first and then join me here."

My jaw dropped, and I used my hand to put it back. I looked away and smiled while her sentence settled in my mind. I was not going to miss this month, and it was all I wanted for Christmas.

My cousin Carmen, me and my cousin Anghelina - selling

"Now, we are going to eat because we didn't eat anything today. Do you want to join us?" mother asked the girls. "We have warm food and also fries and eggplant salad."

She displayed all the plastic containers on the back of the table, opened them all, gave us all forks, and said, "Digg in. I am starving."

Both Cristina and Diana had some fries, as their hands were becoming blueish.

"Guys, go home. Thank you for coming, and I will definitely come to school as soon as I can," I said.

"We will come back tomorrow to see you. Maybe we can bring some food," Diana said.

"Okay, I will be waiting for you," I said, hugging both of them goodbye.

Our last client was around 8:30 p.m., while all other families were getting ready to leave.

"Let me take you home," said one of my older cousins to my mother. "It's getting very late."

"We will find a way, don't worry about us," she said.

When we finally packed our merchandise, there was no one in the plaza. We decided to take a cab because we had made enough money, and there was not a soul on the streets. We took our heavy bags and placed ourselves on the corner of the plaza where there was always traffic, but no cab wanted to stop, seeing us and our immense bags covered in snow. After more than thirty minutes of trying, we decided to walk to the bus stop. Fortunately, a bus picked us up pretty quickly and left us a few streets away from home, and we walked the last few blocks.

As we were getting ready to turn the last corner, my bag ripped, allowing some of the merchandise to fall into the brown snow.

I covered my eyes to stop myself from screaming. I don't know why my legs became heavy, pining me to the ground. I could not leave those items behind because it would mean giving in to the pain of it all. The light on the street was shallow, washing the pavement with a yellow glow. The air was sharp, cutting into any piece of skin exposed.

I took off the bag on my back and placed it on a nearby car, so I could kneel close to where the merchandise fell. Once closer to the ground, I could see there wasn't much to save because the muddy water soaked the cardboard inside the packaging.

"Leave them there, baby. It's okay," said mother.

"I can't," I said.

It took me a while to get them all back because my fingers would not cooperate with me. Trying to get back on my feet, I slipped on my back. Finally, I picked myself up and triumphantly put the dirty merchandise in my pockets.

We walked as if on a frozen lake until we got home. I placed the muddy items in the bathroom sink and took off my shoes. The smell of blood and dirt made my stomach sick.

"Let's wrap your feet in a warm cloth. Hopefully, we will be okay tomorrow," Mother said.

"We will, of course, we will," I said.

The next day, we did it all again.

CHAPTER 12

Marie Claire and the Flea Market

"Rowena, does he know you are a Gypsy?" shouted a group of cousins of mine, in one voice, from a car stopped at a red light while I was crossing the road with a Romanian guy from my college.

"Who, me, a Gypsy?" I said while they drove away.

I blushed and lost my thoughts, dignity, and hope for a good conversation with my first friend from college. He dropped his gaze to the pavement and didn't say a word all the way back to the subway station. We barely said "goodbye" when we arrived at the station where I got off, and since then, we have never hung out together anymore. I was lucky because Clara, one of the girls in my class, decided she would be my friend whether I wanted it or not. Clara and Anca, who were already close, became the only people in college I spent time with during those three years because they were the only ones who saw beyond my ethnicity.

College's first year was an extension of high school, only with no homework and, therefore, more time to spend at the flea market, selling the same merchandise. My mother procured a permanent table at a flea market close to the garbage site. That was her job, while mine was to go every morning to The Dragon to stock on merchandise, go to some classes and then come back to help her out and get us back home.

In my second year, everybody around me got a job, either as an intern or a permanent job, especially those coming from other parts of the country who needed to support themselves. My existing job at the flea market did not make enough, so having a better-paying role was crucial.

I applied for many jobs and interviewed for months, and as soon as they saw me, something changed in their speech and their way of looking at me. I knew what discrimination was, and I always stood up for myself when someone called me names. It was much more difficult when no one said anything, and they left me with doubt. I hated my voice and my Gypsy accent, just never my skin because it reminded me of my father. The last time I was called names, in high school, I almost got into a fight with a guy twice my size, and the only reason I backed off was that I got the chance to curse him in every way I possibly knew, without him saying anything back to me because other people were holding him back. I couldn't curse the interviewers who would look up and down at me in their perfect clothes, perfect skin, and perfect makeup, announcing that someone would call me back.

"That's why we will never be like them." I found myself agreeing with my cousin Casi one day, over coffee, at my place, in our tiny backyard.

She had moved in with me and my mother the year I started college, as her household was becoming too crowded due to her siblings marrying and having children.

"It's not because we don't go to school because even if we do, they still won't allow us in their circles," I said.

"I told you," Casi replied, satisfied. "Also, maybe we don't want to get into those circles. Who would want to behave so properly all the time, anyway? I don't know how they can live this way," she added.

"Right, and that's why our mothers call their mothers *The Grand Ladies* and behave as servants around them," I said.

"Hey, you two, what are you talking about?" chimed in my cousin Ramona, who slammed the gate to my house and walked in gloriously.

She took a plastic seat and added it to our folding table.

"Rowena is saying we will never be like the Romanians," Casi briefed her quickly.

"Who wants to be like them? Only her. I sure don't. She is the one who doesn't know who she is. You are a Romani, my friend, and will forever be, regardless of how much you want to fake it," she laughed and changed topics altogether.

It was the first time I actually saw what was happening. I was speechless for hours.

Is it true? Do I want to be like them?

In the community, my two brothers, Raymond and Lucian, were considered to have gone too far from their routes. They got jobs before they finished college in the first corporate companies to ever come into the country. A few years after the revolution in 1989, companies such as Vodafone (Connex at the beginning) or Danone brought their business and needed great salespeople and did not care about anything else but their skills in sales.

My two brothers flourished in this environment, becoming sales directors very soon in their careers. I truly admired them. They both had clean lives, each one with their apartment, wives, and children. I wasn't sure if I wanted the type of life which included separation from our people. Something deep down inside of me knew that if I chose their path, the separation would be inevitable. I had no idea which path was better, and I desperately wanted both worlds to coexist for me.

Still, I needed a job, so given that I couldn't find anything in 2008 when jobs were scarce, and nobody was willing to give me a chance, I asked my brothers to help me. Lucian got me an interview with *Marie Claire* Romania and gave me almost two hundred dollars to buy new clothes and shoes. We could have lived for a month with the money. Still, he made sure I bought the nicest clothes by taking me personally to a mall. At the end of the shopping session, I could almost pass as a tanned Romanian girl. It was September, so it was believable. I worked on my Roma accent a lot before the interview by listening to Romanian shows on YouTube and recording myself speaking in the same way. I forced myself to adjust my "s" and my "t" specifically and made sure I stopped using slang words.

On the day of the interview, I put on the nice clothes my brother bought for me, practiced my speech, and went in there standing as if I was the smartest and most elegant woman in the world. Faking was what I knew best, given that I had been selling fake merchandise since I was a little girl. My confidence was electric, I believed, taking the elevator to the fifth floor, where Sanoma Hearst reception was. I was greeted by one of the editors of *Marie Claire* and taken to a room where I first met Mara—the chief editor. Although her position was intimidating, to say the least, I found her eyes trustworthy, her voice calm, and her attitude fair. That's what I saw, or at least what I wanted to see. The idea helped me cope with the extreme dissonance between my life and the office I walked it.

"So, how do you deal when subjected to stressful situations?" Mara asked at one point.

"Define stress, please," I said.

The corner of her lips moved up. "You know, when you have strict deadlines coming up, and nothing is ready," Mara said.

"To feel stressed, it would take much more than a deadline. Maybe if our magazine published the wrong article or we were facing bankruptcy is when I would start to feel stressed. Otherwise, anything is manageable," I said.

I am not sure if it was that or something else to get me the job of photo editor for *Marie Claire*. In a few months, I became friends with a part of the editorial team and learned a bit more about what Romanians are like.

The Dragon was where I would still start every single day, at 5:00 a.m., stocking up merchandise for my mother, and the flea market was where I would end every single day, after work or college, to help mother wrap up the day and go home by tram.

"Rowena, is that you?" I heard two voices shouting one day from a car trying to park in the small parking lot of the flea market as I was putting on my big golden earrings.

It was a warm Friday afternoon. I had finished working at 6:00 p.m. and was crossing the parking lot, coming from the subway, to get to my mother's table. As soon as I got out of the subway, I took off my suit jacket, put it in my backpack, loosened up my T-shirt, placed my hair into a bun, and put on my earrings. I couldn't look too Romanian at the flea market, or my cousins would make fun of me, so I would transform as much as I could with just a few touches. The voices were of the stylist working for the magazine and her boyfriend—our product photographer. My Gypsy style was on, and there was no way for me to avoid them, so I faced the problem straight on by approaching their car.

"Yes, it's me. How are you guys?" I said while a car behind them was honking.

"Oh, we are here to do some grocery shopping from the farmers. We were surprised to see you," they said with odd expressions on their faces.

"I am surprised to see you here as well. I hope you find what you need. See you on Monday and have a great weekend," I said, giving no explanation.

They both waved and continued in their pursuit to find a spot to park. I picked up my breath, happy that at least no cousin of mine showed up to say something and embarrass me further, and continued on my way.

I arrived at our table, where fleas were all around my mother's head, and she was trying to get rid of them. The smell of the garbage just a few meters behind us was unbearable.

"Go take a walk," I told my mom.

"It smells horrible, and you need a break. I will take your place until we leave."

She got up, not saying a word, her eyelids closing and barely opening up again. I bought a lemon from a farmer nearby and squeezed it into my cold bottle of water. I took small sips to tame the nausea caused by the smell and the heat. Nobody stopped at our table for the same reasons, but at least we tried. We got home around 9:00 p.m., and I spent an hour in the shower trying to scrub the smell from my skin and nostrils, even though the next day, we would be in the exact same place.

I worked at *Marie Claire* for three years while I finished college, started a master's degree, and got married in my community's tradition. During this time, I became close to each and every person working for *Marie Claire* and other magazines at Sanoma. I never shared my life with any of them. At that time, I believed the only way to manage the two worlds I lived in was by keeping them separate, to the extent that I was two different versions of myself in each world. I avoided situations like the one where my college friend never spoke to me after the encounter with my cousins.

I lost any certainty about what defined me or not, which meant no respect for myself. Confidence and security, I learned much later, are rooted in authenticity. Separating myself into two different versions of myself, depending on the hour of the day or the person I was talking to, was the furthest I ever got from being authentic. The lack of security in my life implied a lot of wasted energy in trying to prove myself, trying to please, or trying to keep consistent with the lies.

CHAPTER 13

Women That Kneel to Expectations

By the time I was twenty, all the cousins I had grown up with were married, and some were already mothers and fathers. Although I had suitors who sent their parents to my mother to discuss possible marriage, she always rejected them. I was free to choose whomever I wanted and marry whenever I wanted. There was only one unspoken but DNA-embedded rule: I was going to remain a virgin until the day I got married. The same rule applied to all my girl cousins. Therefore, after eighteen years old, everybody became frenetic about getting married. Some did not last past fourteen years old.

So, at twenty years old, getting involved in a serious relationship became the focus. It was as if before becoming the only bachelorette in my group, I didn't realize my age. My age became a huge burden, always feeling like the fifth unwelcome wheel. Thankfully, I received a message from an ex-boyfriend of one of my cousins, who had only dated her for a week or so. He was tall and was going to school, and it was enough to get my interest.

"He might be okay, although he does gamble too much," I wrote in the journal I started the year we met.

On our first date, I told him about my Romani heritage, and it was all I had to say for him to understand my DNA-embedded rule. This was a major turnoff, of course, for Romanians and therefore, my options to find someone became extremely limited. He was a different type of Romanian, a rare breed, one who grew up in similar conditions to the Roma people and therefore knew us. They know our struggles and limitations because they grow up with similar ideas. So, my rule was not a problem for him. With this settled, we were both aligned, not necessarily in love.

My people accepted him and, in some cases, much more appreciated than me. I saw this as a great sign because even though I was not looking for everyone's acceptance of my ways, which seemed "Romanian," paradoxically, I was looking for acceptance of my Romanian boyfriend among the Gypsies. One year into our relationship, he was more present at weddings, birthdays, and parties among my extended family than I was because I was always studying during my spare time.

That year was crucial because I was finishing college and trying to apply for a master's in London while working eight hours a day at *Marie Claire* and helping my mother at the flea market. I had it all planned out, and nothing was going to stop me from moving to London.

I got my bachelor's degree with a rating of nine out of ten only because my dissertation teacher was extremely tough on me and did not allow me to slouch one inch. She scrutinized every sentence and had me rewrite it multiple times until it was close to what she called perfection. I got the acceptance letter from the school in London a few weeks after. I invited my cousins, my boyfriend, and some aunts to my place to celebrate in my mother's kitchen. I cooked some food, we bought soda, and a cousin brought some cake.

"Finally, fifteen years of school behind me. I can't believe it," I said.

"So why on Earth do you want more?" a cousin asked jokingly.

"It is a good question. And also, why London?" said Camelia, another older cousin, our next-door neighbor. "Aren't you afraid of leaving your mother alone in this house? What if something happens to her? What if she dies alone?"

I saw my mother nodding in acceptance and lowering her eyes.

"You will visit her every day," I joked. "She has three other children, all living close to her, and also, I will only be there for six months, so she will be okay, I am sure," I added.

"Aren't you afraid someone might rape you, all by yourself, in a city you don't know?" said another cousin, almost spitefully. "Who will ever marry you after then?"

I looked at my boyfriend Bogdan, almost out of reflex, and brought my sight back to my shoelaces, now loose.

"Oh, don't worry. Bogdan loves her, so he would take her," said Ramona, patting Bogdan's back.

He did not disagree. I could not say a word, though. I spent the evening pondering my mother's reaction and the possibility of being raped in London. Maybe Bogdan would still marry me, and maybe not. What if I was going to stay alone forever? I wouldn't be able to live with myself. I knew only one woman from our Gypsy community who had never married for whatever reason. She was looked down upon and shown as a bad example to all the girls who did not have prospects and did not accept the solutions their parents would propose. This thought became my obsession.

I dragged my college friends, Clara and Anca, to London to see a city I had never seen before. We found cheap flights and three beds in a shared motel room with no heating. The weather was at its worst during the few days we visited, and the possibility of being raped seemed more obvious than ever, given how gray and unfriendly this city seemed. We also visited the campus of the school where I was accepted, and it was small and unappealing. Or at least that's how I wanted to see things. I left London and decided I couldn't do it because the city was indeed dangerous, and I probably wasn't good enough to make it on my own.

"I don't know why I dreamed about this so much. I was stupid. I can't do it." I told the girls on our plane back to Bucharest.

A burden lifted from my shoulders just saying it. Now I could accept who I was and stay in my lane, which was much easier than fighting all the voices around me. I would still continue my studies, doing a master's degree in Bucharest. This way, I could comply with the expectations, and I wouldn't completely betray myself. Although I was 90 percent there. I read in a book that courage is the threshold between a meaningless and meaningful life.

Bogdan's patience was, of course, wearing off, and all my aunts, uncles, and cousins were continuously asking when will we get married in our tradition.

As I had just decided I wasn't going anywhere, I agreed there was no reason for me to wait anymore. We had no money for a wedding or for rent. Still, we started planning and telling people.

Everybody was thrilled, although Bogdan's mother knew better about how mentally prepared we both were. I was twenty-two years old, and him twenty-three. We had not fully developed our personalities. A few years later, when we grew up, our values barely overlapped. She tried to warn us, but we already made the decision. The only person who was truly disappointed was my older brother Raymond, who wanted me to follow my dreams. As the Romanian saying goes, *you can harm someone without their permission, but you can never do good to someone against their will.* So, I did not follow his advice to wait a few more years.

That summer was the first since I was seven when I wasn't studying, and mother did not want me at the flea market for once, so I was able to organize the party, although I had no idea what I was doing.

"I wish we could do something really small, at the seaside," I told my sister about the wedding.

"Well, the entire community wants to participate in your marriage, so it won't be an option," she said.

"At least I don't have to do the actual official marriage, thank goodness. I don't even want to call myself a wife in front of people outside of this community," I confessed.

"You still have to do the other thing after the party. You will do it, right?" she asked, her eyes widening with curiosity.

The other thing she referred to was what my community called marriage: proving the loss of virginity on the night of the marriage. The way to do it was by showing a piece of cloth stained with blood, as most girls bleed the first time they make love. This was far less grotesque than what happened during my grandmother's time when they would rape girls into marriage. For her sister Cosilda, the same piece of cloth served as proof of being stolen and locked into the marriage.

Nowadays, girls don't get raped into marriage anymore, and the tradition of the stained towel is at its most modern stage, as one only has to show the actual cloth to the community. Before, the mother-in-law would stand outside the door of the room where the married couple made love for the first time, would come in at the end to check the fabric, and then give the news to our people.

There was no real catalyst to drive this change in time. This is the way of the community to adapt to the changes happening in the world. Although we are closed to society, and we keep our ways, some influence still happens.

In my case, I was going to bring the piece of cloth back home to my mother.

"Yes, of course, I will do it. Imagine the shame if I would not?" I answered my sister's question.

According to our rules, the day before the "marriage," we just party, and on the second day, the couple shows the proof, and then they are declared married. The official marriage, resulting in a marriage certificate, has no value for my community, so we don't do it. I was happy with not really getting married because it was not what I wanted.

As I had no idea how to organize the party, my aunts, uncles, and cousins were there every step of the way, doing the harder work for me. One thing is for sure among my people: when one of us really needs help, we are there for each other unconditionally. One older cousin took care of everything related to drinks, another one negotiated the music, another one the menus at the restaurant, aunts helped my mother prepare the house, and together they made it happen, led by my brother Lucian.

On the second day, I brought the cloth to my mother. This mighty woman, tall and strong in the face of all pain, almost collapsed on her back, and my godfather had to keep her from fainting. Her beautiful eyes were now turned to tiny dots, dripping with tears, and her hands clasped on this piece of fabric symbolizing so much for her. Her red cheeks were now bloodless, and for the first time, I observed the deep wrinkles on her forehead and around her lips. I watched her transform and let out a loud cry of happiness.

As much as I struggled, I could not stop my tears from covering my eyes and chest. A taste of metal and the smell of clogged plumbing made my stomach turn while my limbs remained motionless as people around were rejoicing.

"Nothing I ever did made her so proud. How is it that this piece of cloth brought her so much joy?" I asked my sister the next day.

"Well, you made her proud with this, so be happy," she answered, trying to console me.

To this day, I cannot shake the image out of my mind. How could a mother attribute the entire worth of her daughter to her compliance with someone else's rules? How could I have done the same to myself, accepting my worth came down to a stained towel? This is what I would ask myself for months. Eventually, I had to put the taste of metal and the smell of clogged plumbing away to continue with life, as was expected of me.

Finally, I was truly part of the community, again invited to all the gatherings, a member of honor who kept the rules.

At work, though, I still got to act as myself: a twenty-two-year-old girl doing her thing, just like any other young person my age.

Back home, my role was of a married woman, with all the necessary responsibilities and, hopefully soon, a mother. The gap between my two personalities was deeper than ever before, changing in the blink of an eye on the subway from the business district to Bogdan's mother's place, where we lived. It only got deeper every time someone at work would talk badly about the Roma people, and I would swallow my pride and smile.

Or, when one of my cousins would get beaten by her husband with a chair, and I had to swallow everything I stood for and accept their ways because *they had to educate some women*. The gap became a deep void into which I would just fall into and stay there, at the bottom, for days.

CHAPTER 14

Last Martisor

On my birthday, when turning twenty-four, on my way home from a fair close to Bucharest, I stopped at the first church I saw and ran in.

My new normal now was working at *Marie Claire* and, in my spare time, selling jewelry at different fairs around the city, just like my mother used to. The church was empty, as it was a Sunday evening, and I kneeled at the altar entrance, forgetting myself there for hours.

"Child, are you in danger? Can I help you?" a priest asked when he finally heard my sobs from inside the altar.

I couldn't feel my legs anymore, so I wasn't able to raise up and leave, so I remained kneeling, turning my face to him, and all I could say was, "I don't know, Father. I don't even know."

It was the truth, I had no idea why I was there and what I wanted, but something was clearly wrong. He gave me his blessing and told me to pray for peace of mind.

I left as fast as I could.

"I have work tomorrow. I have to get home soon," I said to no one and searched for the bus station.

Bogdan and I moved in with my mother for me to take care of her. I transformed my old bedroom into a small apartment with its own bathroom and separate entrance. We shared everything else with my mom.

"Your mother brought four of her cousins home today, and they would not leave. I couldn't even go into the kitchen to eat," said Bogdan as soon as I walked in.

"I will speak to her, don't worry," I said, trying to calm him down.

"Rowi, come here," mother shouted from her room.

I opened the door to our room, crossed the small hallway, and walked into her bedroom.

"What?" I asked.

"I need you to give me some money for tomorrow, for the market. How much did you make today at the fair?" she asked.

I gave her half of what I had made and turned back to leave.

"Wait, did you cry? Your eyes look different" her voice became softer, and her eyes deepened.

"Me? I never cry, remember?" I said and fixed her eyes for a minute.

"Not since you were a kid," she said. I kept staring at her until she lowered her eyes.

I walked back to my bedroom.

In the morning, I put on my only good pair of jeans, a white sweater, and my now four-year-old coat Lucian bought for me when I started at *Marie Claire*, and went to work. Walking into the *Marie Claire* office, where everything was clean and organized, was a relief. Where we lived, outside the bedroom, everything was a mess, as our house was always a revolving door for our cousins and aunts.

A colleague suggested we go to a nearby restaurant for lunch as it was payday. Having someone else cooking for me was still a privilege I did not take for granted. While they were ordering, I was improving my knowledge of what is proper to do at such a restaurant or not by observing the others while I continued engaging in the conversation.

"So, I have amazing news! I secured a few spots at the Fashion Week in Milan! I am so pumped. Who is coming with me?" one of my colleagues said.

I was speechless. I had learned what Fashion Week was from my editor in chief, Mara, and I never thought I would attend, given who I was. I never even dared to dream.

"I am going," I said out of nowhere. I was sorry I said it as soon as I heard it.

"Yeah, I can't," said the other colleague, who had already been a few times.

"You go, Rowena, you've never been, and you have been working for *Marie Claire* for four years now," she said.

"Wait, when is it?" I asked.

"February 22–28. Why? You don't have to take off because this is work, so don't worry," my colleague said.

The day of Martisor (the celebration of the beginning of spring) is the first of March, when everyone and their mothers wear a broach as a way to celebrate. Therefore, my community makes thousands of broaches by hand and sells these on the streets in the last week of February. Mother handmade them in January, so I needed to sell them on the streets those days, not attending Fashion Week in Milan.

"Let's figure out budgets, and if it's not too expensive, I am in," I surprised myself again.

"It's mostly covered by the magazine, so don't worry about money," he said.

A rush of joy filled my mind and soul, and for the first time in a long time, I wasn't going to fight it down. I was going to make it work. The other colleague was scrolling her phone while we were finishing our plans.

"Did you guys hear about this Romanian opera singer who died today?" she asked.

"Oh wow, no. How did it happen?" both asked in one voice.

"She had cancer, and she did not win the battle. It makes me so mad. Why do only the good people die, and all the Gypsy singers who kill us with their loud music live happily for so many years?" she asked.

Just as I was taking the last bite of a pasta dish, my stomach closed. I did not even look at her and just stared at my empty plate until the nausea disappeared. The three of us walked back to the office as if nothing had happened because, in their minds, nothing did. I was the only one with a fire in her stomach and an ache in her heart.

As soon as I got home, I burst into my mom's room and said, "Mom, the week of February 22–28, I have to work, and work is sending me to Milan," I lied.

"And are they paying, or how will you do it?" she asked in a calm voice, keeping her eye on what she was holding in her hands

"Yeah, for the most part, they are paying," I said.

"And what are we going to do with the Martisor? Who will help me take our merchandise daily to the plaza where we rented our table? I need someone to drive me there. Can Bogdan help?" She cocked her head, waiting for what she knew the answer would be.

"Maybe some days, but you know we can't rely on him every day. I'll pay someone to use my car, take you there, and bring you back. I can come back early morning on the twenty-seventh so that I won't miss the most important days," I offered.

"All right, if you have to work, you have to. What can we do?" she finally agreed, adding more glue to the piece she was working on: a flowered pin for the Martisor.

Milan's sky was a velvet red when we landed. I was observing my chest and chin rising and my walk changing to match the confident walk of people in the airport. Everybody was gorgeous, everywhere, even in the supermarket close to the hotel where we stopped to buy water. I could close my eyes and listen to them speak about anything, their language being music to my ears. I woke up early because I wanted to go see the Duomo, even from the outside. The Duomo was closed, the plaza was empty at 8:00 a.m., and it was below freezing point, but still I was exhilarated.

I found a McCafé in front of the Dumo and went in to get a coffee. I ordered an espresso and sat inside at a counter whose window overlooked the plaza. The sun was peaking, and I was playing with a ray, caressing my spoon, when I felt taken outside myself. I was looking down from the ceiling at myself and the McCafé staff. What I perceived was something I never did before: compassion.

When I came back to my senses, I wrote in my journal that I was now carrying with me everywhere, 'You are brave all the time.' I closed the journal and tried to imagine, for the first time, life the way I truly wanted, in my deepest dreams, and the word which kept on popping up in my mind was "freedom." I had no idea what freedom meant outside of my world, and not even if I was truly brave or if I would ever be. I did not care. I knew those words were now with me and would become my guides when I needed them. I took my stuff and walked back to the hotel to get ready for the first fashion show of my life.

I learned from our fashion designer at *Marie Claire*: the weirder a piece is, the more expensive it is. That's the best she was able to do to translate fashion trends for me, who said,

"And someone would pay for this shoe thousands of dollars, instead of giving it to someone poor?" when I first saw Yves Saint Laurent.

When the show started, I was left breathless.

"Breathe and close your mouth," my colleague whispered, seeing my reaction.

The models resembled walking pieces of art. Every inch of their bodies was perfect. The runway was long, and the people attending dressed weirdly. I had zero clue about the history of the craft. The only thing I could appreciate was that someone had a story in their mind when they designed each detail of a piece of clothing. At the end, a petite Asian woman dressed in baggy jeans came out on the runway, and everybody gave her standing ovations. I was as displaced as an igloo on a beach. I wanted to crawl outside and run back home.

"Bravo," I said, clapping as strongly as I could, as if my claps were as important as everyone else's.

On the twenty-seventh at 5:30 a.m. I left for Bucharest. I only passed by the home to leave the luggage and put on my *selling on the street* clothes and was at my table before noon. I found the table surrounded by people trying to buy our stuff, unbothered by the muddy and icy water that soaked their feet as the snow melted, and our spot was the place where the drainage of the street would end. My mother was wearing rubber boots, her lips were purple, and her voice was loud and demanding, making people throw their money at her just to get their hands on some of the pieces we created.

The mob dissipated only after 8:00 p.m., so we were exhausted when we got home.

"Tomorrow is the last day. I hope it will be as good as this one," said my mother after we took a shower and settled in our pajamas and warm robes.

"Mom, for me, tomorrow is the absolute last day. I won't be doing this again next year or any year. I know we make money, but I studied enough to make enough money in other ways. I can't be a seller on the streets my entire life," I said, watching her pupils becoming bigger and bigger.

She lit up a cigarette, not saying a word, and I kept silent while staring at her.

"I knew this day would come. I just did not believe it would be so soon. If that's your decision, I understand," she said almost in a whisper.

I looked at her now small frame, crouched on the sofa, as she was smoking, and said in one breath.

"I will make sure we both are financially safe, Mom, I promise. Just not like this anymore," I said.

She nodded and waved her hand instead of saying good night. I kept my word in every way.

PART THREE
BRAVE HEART

CHAPTER 15

The Depth of Our Howls

How can I recreate for you the darkest moment of my life? Let's appeal to your imagination. Close your eyes and see the voices, the silence, the smell of fear, and the depth of our howls.

"He is dead, Giovani is dead," I hear a raucous voice I don't want to recognize. "Can you hear me? Speak to me!"

I get out of bed and sit up, misplaced in my body. I take the phone away from my ear and put it in front of my face to see who it is. The letters are there. It is my cousin Ramona, she is real.

"This is real," I tell myself as I glimpse at Bogdan's body, still asleep, next to me.

I take a deep breath, and I muster some courage to speak.

"Giovani, you mean our Giovani? Giani's Giovani?" I ask, invisible still.

"Yes, he is dead! There was an accident. Casandra and Remus helped the ambulance, and now he is in the morgue. We have to go come pick me up!" Ramona said.

I hung up. I walk outside the house and cross the road. I need to scream. As the warm air of May 3, 2013, hit my face, I feel the urge to vomit my guts out. I try. I can't.

"Should I call someone? I don't know what to do. How do I tell my mom?" I say out loud.

I take a look at our house from the outside, and, for some reason, I see my gate for the first time in years, realizing this is the reusable type they use on construction sites. Like with everything else, we just got used to having a shabby gate, so it's been there for decades. Its rusty color is scratching the inside of my stomach, making me convulse at the idea of going back in to tell my sixty-seven-year-old mother that her twenty-year-old nephew is dead. She has been waiting for death for seventeen years, almost the same time he was alive. I disappear and, unfortunately, appear again, now in front of her bed.

I touch her light skin, kissing her arm gently as if this was the most normal morning of our lives.

"Mom, can you wake up? I am not feeling well," I said.

Her entire being is up in a skip of a beat.

"Another bad dream? Let me put on my shoes. Let's make coffee," she said.

Two more moments, and she is showered and ready to make me coffee.

"Mom, there has been an accident," I stutter.

"What are you talking about? You are still in your pajamas. There was no accident. Now sit down," Mom says.

"Giovani, our Giovani, he is in the hospital." I surprise myself, saying, "We have to go!"

In one clean movement, she sits down and lights a long Kent cigarette.

I walk to my room and open my closet. Bogdan is still sleeping. My vision is blurred. I can't find anything black. I can't wear jeans. They are too tight; people will talk about it. I find a black dress. I put it on with jeans.

"Why black?" my mom asks when she sees me.

"Let's just go," I whisper, taming the nagging nausea back down my throat.

She lost her tears many years ago, so all she has is her voice. She makes a shrill sound, corroded by the despair in her throat. A sound forever imprinted in my memory.

We leave. The smell of a morgue is familiar to me, as we've lost so many souls over the years. Now, juxtaposed with the image of the body of this baby boy, the smell is a punishment for our existence. After bribing the workers there, we manage to smuggle Giovani. It is Good Friday, and morgues are not allowed to release dead people during holidays in Romania. If not for being Gypsies, we would have had to wait until after Easter to take him home. That's not an option in our world. His parents prepare to take him home.

The other young women and I leave to help get the house ready for his arrival. There will be three days of mourning.

The gates to his house open, and we step inside the yard to find a group of elders discussing the best way to divide tasks and start preparing the food, the casket, and the grave. We look at them. They look at us. We don't say anything. At a funeral, you are not allowed to say "hello." You say, "May God rest his/her soul." None of us could yet mutter those words.

It meant all of this was real. One of his aunts was inside, holding a broom in her hands, barefoot. I try to take it away from her, and she falls. I lift her up, and I have her sit on the couch. As her body shakes, I can see the scratches on her face, neck, and shoulders. She whispers something to herself and slaps herself again and again. I leave her there and continue sweeping the floor.

With each new person arriving, there is a scream, someone falls, and someone tears apart their hair or their shirt as they learn about the reality of what they hoped was a misunderstanding.

In a few hours, the house, the backyard, and the streets are full of people waiting for him. Our community, together once again, now to mourn. From the moment he arrives in the casket, throughout the four nights we keep him home, to the day we were buried with him, we all appear and disappear.

One night I stayed up with him and his mother. She had cooked the entire day: his favorite dessert, *cozonac*, for all of us, hundreds of people. The pastry is difficult to make, and women usually bake it only for Easter or Christmas. Watching her head and hands shake while making it was a scene one can't ever forget.

Now, her face contorted and her head shaking continuously, she asks her son, "Please, take me with you."

I look at her and turn my face to his eyes. I close mine to listen to his answer. All I heard was this poisonous smell of embalming fluid and dying flesh. As my chest rose and fell, I kept on listening. The more I listened, the more I perceived what he was trying to say. I kept on listening until the morning, two fingers on my wrist, checking my pulse.

The day we buried him, the sun was screaming at us. I wanted to get out of his way, but I couldn't. I placed myself at one corner of the hole they dug for the casket so I could keep my eyes on him every second. At the graveyard, we stay for hours, his parents not wanting to let him go. They leave, convinced only by the elders to allow Giovani's soul to rest.

The smell of dirt and my own sweat soaked my clothes, pinning me to the ground, and even if I could not feel my legs sitting under me, I did not move. I watched how they closed the casket and lowered it inch by inch. As I watched, with my cousins scattered around, something inside me also took a last breath.

After the burial, we all went back to his home, where the women who stayed behind had prepared dinner for everyone. The plates were ready, and people were sitting in their chairs, being served, not saying a word. Kids were not playing, the wind had stopped completely, and the young people were not talking to each other. Even the cars stopped appearing on the street. Complete and utter silence was bestowed upon us, following us for the rest of our lives.

I wasn't able to sleep that night due to the guilt for being alive and shame for sleeping in my peaceful home when Giovani's parents felt crushed.

As the blueish light of dusk made its way through my curtains while my numb body pinned itself to the chair in my room, I couldn't help but ask the question, "Why bother to live?"

I started reflecting on my past and my future, and my choices. For the first time, it hit me how far from freedom I was. The realization scared me even more. I stood up and took my journal to write down these thoughts and see their shape on paper. A few pages in, and I was able to assess, with my control freak part of the brain, that I was losing it. For the first time, it did not bother me. I wanted to lose all of it.

By this time, at twenty-five, I had moved from *Marie Claire* to work with my brother Raymond who had a consulting company. We wrote grant requests for European funding for companies and individuals in Romania. I was happy to spend twelve to fourteen hours a day just working, sometimes coming back in the morning from work. I didn't drink alcohol, smoke, or do drugs. Work was what I did to stop the torture of these thoughts, which in a few weeks had become a snowball so big it could swallow me entirely. They robbed my sleep, my mornings, my peace, and some of my relationships. I was lucky my brother was seeing me every day, and although we didn't work directly together, it was obvious I was not myself.

One Sunday morning, he took me out for a serious talk at a coffee shop close to home. A lot of words were coming from his mouth, whereas I could barely catch a few, nodding and making sure I made eye contact. I took a deep breath and choked on the remorse for the sadness I saw in his eyes for not getting through to me. So I allowed myself to let out one sentence:

"Why care when death can take it all away any day, and all that is left is a corpse that disintegrates?" I asked.

His pupils shrunk all of a sudden. He took a sip of his coffee, straightened his back, and said, "As humans, we are all so small, as a drop in the ocean. But don't forget, we are also the ocean if we open our hearts. No, life has no meaning when you live your life from your mind. Think about it this way: What is the meaning of the love we have for each other? The love you feel for your mother? There is no meaning. Love just is. So is life. We give it meaning by living it at our best, allowing ourselves to be who we really are, free from the definitions of others. We are the ones who give it meaning; remember this."

The tears I previously could not tame while he was talking, finally stopped. Something inside me woke up, someone I hadn't made acquaintance with. I hugged my brother as if it was the first time I had seen him in years because it was. Walking home, this new person who woke up in me grew legs and won space over my old self, and I allowed it.

"There is nothing to be afraid of anymore," I heard myself whispering to no one.

When I got home, I was happy to see I had the place to myself. It was May, and the summer had started early. There was a feeling of staleness everywhere. I opened all the windows, pulled open the curtains to let the sunshine in, and breathed in new air, an air of hope. I opened my laptop and Googled "scholarship for master's degrees" and opened an Excel to start my research of possibilities. The bark of our neighbor's dog, the birds chirping, people visiting my mother, and the sound of the big old gate opening and closing many times, nothing moved me. It was dark when I got up from the chair, satisfied with my list of ideas.

CHAPTER 16

The Lord Is My Shepherd

How do you know when life is about to change drastically? Sometimes it's obvious, and other times it's the day when you decide to bake a cherry pie on a hot summer day.

I was in my mother's kitchen, watching the blueish color of the oven transforming the dough. The four walls, formerly the kingdom of my grandmother Gutuia became my terrain. Outside, kids played hide-and-seek, turning my thoughts back to my happiest days before I became a woman. Since we didn't have air conditioning, we opened all the windows, so the smell of our neighbor's dogs was mixed with the sour-sweet smell of cooked cherries. My cheeks were burning from the oven heat when my cousin Casi appeared at my door, sweaty, tired, and visibly eager to talk to me.

"Can we go outside, to the park in front of your house, to talk? You are mad for baking now in this heat. What were you thinking?" she said, annoyed, walking outside, expecting me to follow.

I had just finished, so I wrapped the pie in paper and went out to meet her.

"What happened? Are Giovani's parents okay?" I asked.

"Yes. I am here for a different reason," she said, straightening her back and lifting her chin.

Her eyes melted, deepening, and the little smile she showed disappeared under her now perched lips.

"You are nervous, and you are making me nervous. Tell me what's happening," I said.

"Okay, look, you have to swear you will never say I told you this. Swear it to me now," she said.

"What is it? Tell me," I won't say anything, I promised.

"Well, now I can see you are different, acting as if nothing else can hurt you after Giovani died and wanting to leave the country to study. Now I can tell you. You see, it has been going on for years, and no one told you. Your partner has been hooking up with different women all the time. I saw the messages between him and my husband. He is taking advantage of you, using you to help him, and he doesn't really love you. He is with you because you are always there and will always be, regardless of what he does. He actually said those words. I saw it in a message he sent. If you can, let him go," she said.

I wanted to run away and pretend I hadn't heard. My eyes fell to the ground, and my voice was so shallow I couldn't even hear myself when I asked her, "Are you sure it was him? There are other people with his name in our group," I tried.

"Rowi, of course I know it's him," she said. She stayed with me for a few more hours. I don't remember anything else from the conversation. I wanted her to stay with me so I wouldn't end up at home thinking about this by myself. After a few hours, she had to go.

That night, he was out, and he didn't come home until the morning, which gave me time to reflect. I opened my journal and asked the question: *Should I want to be really free or just have some freedom?*

It caught me by surprise to see that instead of being hurt, I felt relief. This situation opened up the possibility for me to think about what I truly wanted to do with my life. *I am the product of whatever everyone else wanted me to be, but could I dare to want something for myself that's very different? But... even the Lord said: "The Lord is my shepherd, I shall not want," so who am I to question everything?* I continued writing.

I decided to wait before deciding to end the relationship, so I pretended as if nothing had happened for a few days while I tried to ask my older cousins if this had ever happened to them. One of them told me her husband had three children with two other women. Another had to beat a woman her husband was dating to scare her off. Another had caught her husband having an affair that lasted many years. Each and every one of them stayed in the relationship mainly because they did not want to have a second husband, as this meant they were not respectable anymore.

"This is nothing. Come on, he doesn't beat you up, he doesn't do drugs, and he works. What else do you want? Keep your head down and show him you are better than any other woman," one of my cousins said.

Another one, forced into a second marriage after her husband left her, resulting in a painful life, said, "Don't ever leave him, you hear? You are a Romani woman. You are a righteous Gypsy woman, so keep your husband. You hear me?" she said, barely catching her breath.

The second day I woke up wondering: "If I die tomorrow in a car accident, would I be sorry for leaving or staying? What decision would be harder to accept?"

We broke up the same night. I did not shed one tear, and for the first night in years, I slept the entire night.

When I woke up, the first thing I did was open my laptop and check for emails from the many scholarships I had applied for. After my last failure with London, I had set my eyes on Paris because my brother Lucian lived there for a few years, working for a company. In Paris, I found a twelve-month master's degree in international project management at École Supérieure de Commerce de Paris, taught in English, which had built in a month-long trip to Asia to study the same topic at a partner school. My heart would shrink and explode simultaneously, just dreaming about studying in this prestigious school.

My journal was now full of daydreaming, where I would try to imagine a day in my new life, with all the details: Where would I eat? How would I behave? How would I dress? The price and cost of living were as far from my possibilities as Earth is from Neptune. The scholarship was my only solution, and so far, nothing was materializing. My hopes were falling apart.

One morning, though, my laptop showed a message I could not believe.

Right there, on my screen, it said, "Accepted for a fifteen thousand euros grant." I checked for the email address to make sure this was not a scam. I jumped up from my seat and returned in a split second back to the screen, biting my nails while reading again and again.

"Is this true? I need certainty before I get too excited," I said.

I had never seen so much money put together and would never hope to own such a fortune and use it to pay for school.

So I called the phone number in the email.

"Hello, Mr. M.? Is this you? I'm Rowena, I got an email from you saying you will be my officer for my scholarship, and I was accepted. Is this you?" I asked, trying not to sigh.

"Hello, Rowena. Yes, it is me," the voice on the phone said.

"Is this true? Was I accepted?" I continued my list of questions without inhaling.

"We accepted you. It is correct," I heard.

"Mr. M., are you sure? This is Rowena Marin. I'm a Gypsy," I said out of nowhere.

"Yes, dear, I know who you are, and of course, you are a Roma. This is why you got the scholarship. Now I have to go. We will keep in touch, thank you," he said, hanging up.

My entire body was now jumping on the bed like a kid.

"I am a Gypsy, I am a Gypsy, and I am a scholar, and I am a scholar," I started singing while jumping.

There was always this want in me to be the first Romani woman in my community to do things: finish college, work for a multinational company, travel the world, do a marathon, and be outstanding. My family raised me to consider these things a sin toward my community, my family, and even God because he specifically said He was our shepherd and "we shall not want."

My mom and my community did not want what was best for me if that did not include them. Never questioning their wants and only mine, I allowed myself not to become who I am, which is the worst sin of all. I would only understand this many years later, and still, somehow, I accepted myself as a sinner and an outcast because *there was nothing to be afraid of anymore.*

CHAPTER 17

Who Am I?

The leaves were dying, the Euro was in steady decline for the first time after replacing the peseta, and I arrived in Madrid.

The street was pitch black, so I decided to call my brother back home to walk with me. He did not pick up. Every woman in my community knows this: *never walk alone.* I was walking on a dark street in a foreign country. Not ideal to not know the language, to think of rape movie scenes, or question my decision to leave the country and go against what my relatives wanted for me.

Save for the huge dog sitting in front of a house, no soul was walking on the street. I was relieved. At least I wasn't going to get raped. Also, the dog didn't speak the national language either. I walked straight to him with confidence in myself and the universe, and as he lifted himself and walked toward me, a lamppost switched on.

I finally saw the sign: "Calle Imerovigli." I arrived in the right place and could see a gate on my left resembling the one I saw in the pictures. I thanked the dog and crossed the road.

I rang the rusty bell and waited, holding close my little suit-case and backpack. A beautiful, taller-than-life woman in her fifties opened the gate, waiting for me with a big smile and a hug. She showed me into a well-lit yard, and I could see white, violet, and pink roses, all wrapped in a lush green scenery. The small trail passed by a pool and a house all made of glass, where many mannequins were sitting in weird positions, naked. I could see walls covered in paintings and a huge cat sleeping on the gray sofa. We finally made it to my studio in her backyard—one long room which served as a bedroom-living room, kitchen, and bathroom, all in one. My brother Lucian's Spanish friend recommended the place as being safe and close to the school. My host disappeared quickly to allow me to settle in. I closed the door behind her and crashed on the tiny sleeper sofa. It took me weeks to start believing in the reality of it all.

ESCP Europe, the school I wanted to attend, did not have any more spots in Paris for the master's I wanted by the time I received my scholarship. So, they gave me the option to attend classes in Madrid. The only Spanish I knew I heard in soap operas during my childhood. I didn't know anybody, and the only Romanian girl from the college, whom I was in contact with before arriving in Madrid, didn't really want to meet me, let alone help me.

Even so, I managed. From the first week of school, I discovered a Rowena I didn't know before, a Rowena I really liked. Courageous, proactive, and the informal leader of my class on various administrative themes, keeping up with the class's level. Sometimes, late at night, after I got home from my classes, I used to stop and think about how, after a full month, no one raped me. Even this fear, which not long before was paralyzing, couldn't stand in my way.

I signed up as part of the organizing team of a Start-up Weekend—an event in which people build a business in seventy-two hours. I signed up for any volunteering on campus and made friends with everyone.

On the last morning of the start-up event, and after a Friday and Saturday consisting of sixteen-hour workdays, I waited for the bus with such a huge joy in my soul that I couldn't stand still. I found myself dancing in the bus station, alone at 7:00 a.m.

When the bus driver arrived, he smiled and said, "Me alegraste la mañana, gracias (You made my day)."

I took a seat and finally knew I was on the right path.

"This is what true happiness feels like," I told myself.

One of the women attending the event told me, "Your patience and desire to win motivated me to come today."

I was transforming from a docile child into a woman who could bring joy, motivation, and value to other people.

For the first time in my life, I could stand tall and confident as myself.

The master's consisted of six months of study in Madrid and a month in Asia. I was studying in various parts of the world to expose myself to different cultures. The first stop—Mumbai, where I adapted to the environment after the shock of the first days. I became friends with Shraddha, an Indian girl who studied in England, who had taken me and my colleagues under her wing and showed us around.

Shraddha's mother wanted to show me a market in town where she would test our negotiation abilities. They found it funny to take international visitors to the market because, usually, Europeans aren't really born negotiators, as they are. After twenty minutes of seeing me either deal with the merchants or exchange life stories, she got bored and wanted us to leave. I didn't want to stop. Engaging with the kind traders, I realized I wasn't a Roma to them, and yet I was more myself than ever. There, my ethnicity didn't matter one bit. I enjoyed putting into practice what I had learned among my people: negotiating, reading people, and annoying them to the point where we became friends. I learned I loved discovering the limits of people I was talking to and testing their patience just enough so they wouldn't sense it. I was enjoying the smell of the market, a combination of leathers, spices, cooked food, and dust, and the familiar sound: fuss, market, and salespeople. I was so far away, and yet I was home.

I was enough.

It didn't take long until "who I am" came back to find me, even on a different continent. I was in Beijing on Saint Nicholas Day. For me, Saint Nicholas Day had a bigger meaning than Christmas. It was the name day of my father and the day I used to suffer the most when I was a child. If on Christmas, my folks managed to somehow provide, each year on December 6, we barely gathered food to put on the table.

So far from the people I loved and from familiarity, I decided to post on social media a famous Romanian song that spoke about missing home and feeling stuck between wanting to explore the world and leaving a part of your heart always behind. Although a pop song, the lyrics spoke exactly to what I was living.

My roommate distracted me with some gossip after I posted, but the red little notifications bell started chiming frenetically. Messages were pouring from aunts, uncles, and cousins.

"How can you be so shallow?" wrote one of my cousins.

"You left everything behind to go to Asia, and now you are sorry? It's what you get for being so selfish," was another message.

It kept on coming for a while. I had to close my laptop and go out for a walk.

After a few hours of walking and coming back to my room, I decided to shut the door of my heart to my entire community, at least for a while, until I could figure out how to manage the burden of my inner conflict. I couldn't be myself among them, and I couldn't be a Roma woman in the world. I needed time to get out of my head.

Even in my master's classes, I didn't say anything about my ethnicity because I already had the label of being from

Romania. Some of my colleagues were cautious around me because Romanians had a bad reputation in Spain. They would say Romanian women are only about stealing rich men away from their wives and the Romanian men are only about stealing—anything they could.

I didn't have any advantageous labels: Gypsy, Romanian, a woman.

On the plane back to Europe from Asia, I mustered the courage to write in my journal again and have an honest conversation between different parts of myself that did not agree on who I was and how to behave. After many hours of writing, I came to a conclusion:

I decided I was going to act as myself and nothing more.

Back in Spain, the days and nights of Madrid were magically easy to live. It was as if I was living in a fairytale, with a large smile on my face all the time. Not because everything was going great; before I got a job, there were days when I was hungry, and I had to survive on a maximum of seven to ten euros a day. Still, because I didn't have the pressure of my ethnicity, I was growing wings, although I knew these would get cut as soon as I got home.

Regardless of how important it was for me to fly and how brave I became, something kept me up at night. I didn't want to disappoint my family to the point of no return. Once you experience flying, you don't want to crawl anymore.

CHAPTER 18

Forward or Back?

At 7:00 a.m., on a March day, the Madrid sky looked like a Monet painting, sublime beauty showing itself only for moments to those who had the eye to see it. The colors and the light would transport me to my childhood legends, specifically the moment when I got to the happy ending. Regardless of how my nightmares would torture me during the night, I would wake up every morning to go for a run around Plaza de España, where I lived, to enjoy the feeling of freedom and space I got every time I would run during sunrise. I would always say to my Spanish friends that Madrid has the most beautiful sky in the world.

The first six months of my program had ended, and now it was time for me to find an internship. At the Start-up Weekend I coordinated, I met the founder of a start-up called Nona-box, a subscription model where mothers would receive each month a box of products for their newborns. She offered me an internship in her marketing team with the possibility of a long-term contract. I had no idea about digital marketing, but I knew I could learn anything, so I took it. My Spanish was not perfect yet, although I was reading everything I could get my hands on to ensure I knew how to spell and write correctly. Izanami, the founder, knew this well, and she still trusted me.

On my first day in the office, I heard a colleague announcing to the entire forty-person team in the open space that he was not feeling well and was "*constipado.*" I was absolutely perplexed and stared at him for too many minutes. I knew my Gypsy norms were way off. In my community, it was not polite even to say you had to use the restroom, for a woman especially. Still, by now, I was acquainted with the office norms, and I knew it was not professional to talk about the movement of your bowls in public.

I finally decided to Google the meaning of *constipado* in Spanish. I couldn't help but burst into loud laughter when I understood the guy was saying he felt congested. Eighty eyes were looking at me with curiosity. I told them what happened, and all forty of us had a good laugh.

For the next year, we became a family. The start-up operated in five countries, so we had people from the UK, Italy, Germany, France, and of course, Spain. I was the only Romanian, and for the first time in my life, this was not good or bad, just a detail. The IT boys would ask me sometimes if, after a party, I join the Romanian crew that steels copper from the outskirts of Madrid. However, they had a joke for each of us, and truly mine was the funniest one because I was always falling asleep during parties, movies, or on the subway, so stealing copper after a party would have been hard to do. Every day I learned something new about food from the Italians, funny idioms from the Spanish, art from the French, and music from the Germans.

Coming back to my tiny room in Plaza de España, where only a single bed fit, while my closet had to be in the hallway, in an apartment shared with three other girls, I felt fulfillment. Aurelie Sechet, a French girl who lived there when I moved in, became one of my best friends. Every evening was perfect, as we would explore the city together as two children discovering the world for the first time. I did not want this life ever to end.

One cold February night, I got a call from Anca, one of my best friends. She had left to study in France a few years before me, which inspired me to do what I was doing. We talked for more than an hour, as usual.

Among other things, she asked me, "Rowi, are you happy there?"

"I'm happy anywhere, just not at home. But how much longer can I stay away?" I said.

I don't remember if she answered my question. I didn't know what I was running from, only that I didn't want to go back to who I was before; to a lifestyle loaded with hardship. I was becoming a woman I respected and whom I didn't want to disappoint.

"Which way, which way?" Alice in Wonderland asks herself at one point in the story.

I was stuck there. "Should I disappoint myself or my family?"

I began the following week with this question in mind. It was Monday morning, and I arrived at work with this feeling of *what now?*

I was in the kitchen preparing myself a coffee when the phone rang.

"Rowi, can you talk?" the voice said. It was Loredana, my sister.

"Yes, I just finished making a coffee. How are you? Is everything okay?"

"Yes. I have some big news for you. Sit down if you're standing."

She didn't have to say a word. She'd wanted it for so many years, and it had finally happened: she was pregnant. I spilled my coffee on my pants. I didn't care. I was happy all day. I already had three nephews: a girl and two boys, my brothers' children, whom I adore. But if I were to continue my stay abroad, I would miss seeing my sister's boy growing up. The way home was becoming clearer.

The same week, on Friday, Izanami, the founder of Nonabox, gathered all of us close to the end of the day to make an announcement. This time I wasn't holding a cup of coffee in my hand, which was good because I might have thrown it all on her. The start-up was going to terminate its activity in a couple of weeks due to financial problems, which she had never told us about.

The next day, I ran further than ever before, trying to get rid of the pain in my chest. I couldn't believe the dream had come to an end and I had to go back to Romania. My legs were jogging without me, and I cried the whole time until I stopped in a garden, a place I had never been before. Although it was February, some roses were blossoming. Somehow, the idea of early blossomed roses and maybe the fact I blew off steam made me smile.

Something within me said, "It's going to be okay."

I needed to know that.

And so, the bad sheep of the family returned home. Everything was the same: the same street, the same people, the same jokes, the same existential crisis, the same constant gossip, and the same feeling of heaviness on my shoulders. I didn't have a job waiting for me in Romania, so I decided to work with my brothers, who had just opened a consulting business. I was proud of them, maybe the first and only Gypsies who had managed to do this sort of thing. Me, I wasn't at all proud of myself.

In my life, I was a disappointment to the people around me, but now I have become a disappointment to myself because I had discovered my potential and then thrown it in the trash.

No matter what I did, I couldn't hide as if I had a sign which said *disposable garbage*. I carried it everywhere with me. I didn't share these feelings with anyone because they wouldn't understand. I was the only woman I knew who was on this journey. To Mom and my community, I was *the prodigal daughter* who had come back, so they would forgive me. In the eyes of my siblings, I was the same sister who received their love unconditionally in Spain, Romania, or any other corner of the world I would have chosen.

In my eyes, I was the embodiment of compromise. All of my childhood, I'd had dreams which were hard to understand at such a young age. I had such a dream during the week I returned home, one I understood, but I could not do anything about it.

I dreamed I was on a bike with Mom and an aunt, an old Gypsy lady I hadn't seen in years. The bike was hard to steer, and I could barely keep it on track when a hill I had to climb appeared out of nowhere. I began climbing it, and soon I lost control, so the three of us fell. Mom and my aunt got up and left, but I couldn't due to the pain caused by a bleeding injury.

I woke up saying, "I know, I will fall at some point. But, for now, I need to climb my hill."

Shortly after, I attended my godfather's son's birthday. As usual, the women sat away from the men, joking, laughing, and telling life stories. For the girls who wanted something more from life, I was a role model because I had studied abroad but was *still a Romani woman,* as they used to say. I came back to Mom, to my sister, because I forgave the man who cheated on me, meaning I hadn't completely shaken off the person I was before. Among the elders and conservatives, I had a questionable reputation.

That night it was clear to me who thought what of me because the first group addressed me by "Rowi," and the second group just said, "You." It was a way of setting some kind of distance between me and them, the ones without a stained reputation. But the paralyzing fear of judgment I'd had in the past wasn't there anymore. For the first time, I acknowledged them for what they were: women with admiration or with fear of the unknown. It was about them, not about me. My fear turned to compassion toward them.

Approaching morning, when almost all the men were drunk, we all gathered because it was the last round of barbecue. This particular moment, in which a group of Gypsy men cooks, is maybe the only one in which they show their love for their wives. They invite them to eat with such love and acceptance as if they need approval. *"Hai şeorale te han, că termenisardeam* (Come and eat, girls, the food is ready)," a cousin of mine proudly announced.

We all started eating, maybe twenty people because we're a lot of us when we gather. One of my godfather's boys, older than me, said to a girl, "First, you serve food to your husband, and then you eat, fatty."

It must have just been a bad joke. People were laughing. The girl stood up and placed a steak on her husband's plate, even though the pot was an elbow away from him.

I stood up, smiling, and said to the man who'd made the joke: "Why didn't you get up to serve him if you're so bothered? Or maybe you're just misogynistic? You saw she was already eating. She's also pregnant. Aren't you at least a bit ashamed of who you are and what you represent?"

It got quiet. He didn't respond. I sat down at my seat peacefully and allowed the women (aunts and cousins) to lecture me on how disrespectful it is to talk back to men, especially when they are older than us, regardless of what they say.

I left shortly after and never returned home to my godfather, whom I love. Such a revolt can have serious consequences. I would be spoken ill of and even excluded from certain circles. From that moment, I became a topic of discussion, a bad example for young girls. In some areas, I was disappointed with myself, but I was no longer afraid to say what I believed. Moreover, I realized now that I had a responsibility to say what I believed. I had gained self-knowledge and knowledge of the truth. I was furious at what I realized now was degrading behavior on the part of people I considered authority figures—my older cousins.

With new perspectives and a burning desire to manifest my new personality, I applied for a job at IBM, which I got. I met new people, learned a lot, and made new friends, but still, I didn't tell anyone I was a Romni. I wouldn't have denied it for a second, but I wasn't talking openly about my personal life. I was still living a double life as I had before I left, keeping things separate. Only now, I noticed I was the same person in both worlds.

I became an ambitious woman with clear beliefs, confident in her intellectual capacity, who no longer needed approval. I walked away from most of my past friendships, away from relatives whom I considered toxic, and became an advocate against discrimination.

One time at a Christmas company party, I happened to over-hear a remark by a colleague I barely knew, regarding "filthy manelists" (people singing or listening to Gypsy songs) who refuse to die, whereas other good people do.

It was the same thing I'd heard once from my colleague at *Marie Claire*, and I hadn't had the courage to say anything.

This time I approached the person directly and said, "Look me in the eyes and tell me you want me to die instead of someone better than me. I am a manelist, but not necessarily a filthy one. My cousins are manelists, my uncles are, and my aunts are. Now tell me again what you just said?"

"What do you mean?" he answered, his body facing me but his eyes moving from left to right, searching for a way to escape.

"I think you got a general idea: a Gypsy just overheard what you said. Now, if you really believe what you just said, repeat it." I answered.

He continued smiling while I stared his eyes away from me and into the ground. His group of friends all abandoned him, so I got closer to him and whispered in his ear:

"You have no idea who we are, and you have no right to call us Gypsies. We are the Romani people for you from now on. We deserve as much respect as what I am giving you now, even though you do not deserve it. I hope you learned a lesson today, and I hope you will think deeper in the future before you let out so much resentment in the world."

I took a step back to look at him once more and walked away. From that moment on, he never looked me in the eyes when we met in the company hallways.

When being a woman in the community felt as if being a fifth wheel to a car, and being a Romani in Romania felt as if being the flat tire, my only daily desire was to keep myself in a state where I knew what I stood for and what I didn't and to do my best to stay honest with myself. Sometimes I was strong enough to do it, but most of the time, I wasn't. Most of the time, I was inauthentic and that had consequences.

CHAPTER 19

A Eulogy to My Lost Self

Inauthenticity and lying to oneself kill. It kills courage, desire for life, freedom, and meaning. In my case, it also killed my first pregnancy.

On June nights, my little street fills with children heading to the playground just in front of my rusty gate, as well as many of my relatives who live nearby. The playground becomes a meeting point for people who spend the day selling in flea markets and want to enjoy the fresh air while watching their kids play.

Every time I would go out in the evenings, I tried to spend some time with whoever was there before I left. It would have shown a lack of respect or a sign that I was too important to spend time with my own people if I didn't. One night, all dressed up to attend a business event, I played the part and walked up to the park to say hello before calling an Uber.

One of my older cousins asked me, "Where are you going? Does your partner know you are going to see your boss and other colleagues in the evening dressed like this?"

"My boss and my colleagues are women. There is only one guy who does not like women. He prefers men. Also, my partner lives right there in my house with me and my mother, so yes, he knows. He sees me walking out. There is no problem here," I said.

"Well, he is a saint. I would keep you tied to the bed," she said, looking away.

The Uber dropped me at one of the highest-ranked restaurants in the city. The faux grass at the door looked expensive, the doorman looked like a model, and the hostess greeted me with a glass of Don Perignon.

"Look who's here," said a friend of mine, Cristina, to the people at our table.

"Oh, gosh. Not so loud, Cris. How are you?" I said, trying to smile.

"I am a bit tipsy," she said, grabbing my hand to take me back to our team.

As soon as I got there, I could sense my spine more erect, my head and chest lifting. Someone else took over. My voice became high and clear. I could hear myself offering advice, setting rules, and demanding things from people around me.

I got home late and asked the Uber driver to turn his lights off as we entered the street. I snuck through the gate without anyone seeing me and turned on the bathroom light so I could get into bed. My partner was out, and I had no idea where. My concern was making sure no one in the little park could see my bedroom lights turning on late. I changed and got into the covers safely.

In the morning, I woke up with nausea and vomited all day.

"What did you eat last night?" my mom asked me.

"The usual stuff, salad, and so on," I said.

"Did you drink too much?" she asked.

"One glass of champagne," I said while my stomach wanted to come out of my mouth.

"Well, then you should stop drinking. You are probably pregnant," she said, sure of herself.

"No, I am not!" I answered. For some reason, I just didn't consider the possibility, even for a second.

I told my partner, and we rushed to the pharmacy to buy a test. The pharmacist told me I had to wait until the morning to take it. I spent the rest of the day looking at the big clock in my bedroom. I wanted to hear it ticking, to make sure time was passing by.

I woke up with the sun's first rays through my bedroom window.

"It's time," I said to myself, opening my eyes as if someone had just screamed in my ear to get up.

As I waited for the results, I closed my eyes, trying to forget who I was, even for a few minutes. My heart was on the floor, my body heavier than ever, my mouth dry, and my nostrils barely allowed air into my lungs. Each breath was more painful than the last. My chest felt glued to my back.

My eyelids opened beyond my will, driven by pure curiosity, to see the two lines as red as they could possibly be. Alone in the bathroom the size of a small closet, I rose above my body and placed myself in a corner, safely, where I could see my hands covering my eyes and tears falling on my neck. My sighs weren't allowing me time to breathe, so my breaths turned to coughs, which sounded like an old car's engine. I only stopped once I realized I had to tell people around me. I managed to regain control, now back in my body, and emerged from the bathroom to tell people what they would become: a father, a grandmother, and an uncle. As I shared the news and the shock wore off, I became more and more excited, gaining consciousness of the beautiful gift given to me: becoming a mother.

"This baby is mine," I heard myself telling my sister, who was pregnant in her last trimester.

"What do you mean?" she asked.

"Well, I am going to raise it the way I think is best, and no one else can tell me what to do," I said.

"Well, maybe your partner will have some say in the deal," my sister tried.

"I asked him, and he said it is fine with him for me to make all the decisions," I said.

"Oh wow, that's good then," she said, clearly not believing a word.

He did agree.

The first medical appointment confirmed the pregnancy and informed me I was already in my second month. A few days later, the entire community knew. I received many: "it's about time" from people, and on every occasion, I smiled politely and nodded while clenching my fists.

Some days I talked to my belly, preparing myself and whatever I had inside for a lifetime of connection. I would share my secrets, whisper my thoughts, and caress the skin, hoping it would help the growth.

"You are now a seed. Seeds need love, too, to become flowers. So I will bathe you in love to make sure you blossom," I used to tell it while driving to work in the mornings.

Some days, when people called me to ask me about my pregnancy, I wanted to laugh and say the rumors were not true.

"What do you mean? I am not even married, and I am too young anyway." That is what I wanted to say.

Soon I would remember: it could not be that the Gypsy Rowena was going to have a baby while the free and independent Rowena, who had a career to follow, was not going to. Right there and then, the two worlds I kept separate had to collide and crush each other.

A few weeks later, I had another routine check-up. I chose to attend the practice of the same doctor Lori, my sister, attended throughout her pregnancy. My appointment was early in the morning on a Saturday. When I woke up, I giggled, knowing it would be the moment I would hear the heartbeat of the person growing inside me.

The smell of bleach was drowning the dark waiting room, and my feet were ready to run away back to Madrid, where life was easy. I pulled the curtains to let some air in, but the windows did not open. My stomach sent me signs of nausea that I repressed so hard as if to punish myself.

Finally, the obstetrician invited me into her office and showed me the table where I was supposed to sit and wait for her investigation.

"This will be a bit uncomfortable," she added before she started the ultrasound. She smiled.

I smiled back, hopeful.

I could see only the corner of her face when I noticed her jaw dropping. She continued to move her hand on my body, searching, looking at the monitors, and making no eye contact with me.

I closed my eyes and prayed to hear something coming out of those monitors.

"I believe…" I heard her say.

I asked nothing.

"I believe it did not make it. I am sorry. Sometimes it happens. Sometimes, especially the first pregnancies, can result in the sudden death of the fetus at an early stage," she said without blinking.

"I am so sorry!" she added, pulling away from me.

"What do you mean? It is not born. How could it die? Search more, search more," I said as loud as I could.

Looking back at myself, I now know my body could not grow a life inside itself because it could barely keep me alive. My psyche was convulsing due to my inauthenticity, and I was weak. I was so disappointed with myself that I hated every inch of my body. For some who feel similarly, life goes on. For some of us, as much as we want to, it doesn't. That day it stopped.

"Madam, I am so sorry. This can happen," she said.

She started explaining how often this happens, and this was more common than I knew, but people don't talk about it.

"Stop talking," I said as I got dressed, with my gaze blurred, my nose running, and my hands shaking.

"You think I care this happens often? I don't. This *was my* baby," I said.

She lowered her gaze and turned her back on me.

I left her practice, barely able to stand. I wasn't able to drive back. Since it wasn't far from home, my feet started walking. I stopped at every lamppost to catch my breath. I fell once, tripping on something I didn't see because my gaze was too blurry. Someone picked me up and offered me some tissues. From there, I was able to get home, making sure I touched things on my way, preventing another fall.

More than two hours later, I arrived at my bed and crawled in. I took some painkillers and fell asleep.

I woke up the next day to a dozen of missed calls from my sister. My head was spinning, and the skin on my chest was burning. Still, I called Lori back.

"Rowi, what happened? Is it true?" she asked, crying.

Before crashing into bed, I only muttered these words to my partner: "It is dead."

So he told my mother, who informed my sister.

I wanted to say something to Lori that wouldn't worry her too much. Nothing came out of me.

All I could mutter was: "Yes, it is true."

"What is happening with us? I am in the hospital as of this morning. There is something wrong with my pregnancy as well," my sister said.

"What do you mean? What did they say? What is wrong? Which hospital are you in?" I asked, as somehow all the words in the world came back to me.

Still, with a terrible migraine and nausea, I forced myself out of bed to see her at the hospital. I left my pain behind, and thirty minutes after her call, I was holding her hand by her bed.

They didn't know why, but her baby stopped growing.

She gave birth to Patrick at seven months, so he initially needed a lot of medical help. She spent the next year in hospitals to save his life.

After that day, I chose not to think about what had happened to me at all. When my family, friends, or community tried to bring it up, I would shut them down quickly. It was too much for me to understand or accept.

To my sister and my two brothers, I wanted to say, "I killed this baby with my lies." I could never say these words to anyone.

I wrote them down in my journal one night, waking up from a nightmare.

"Will I ever be able to climb out of this?" I added.

"Should I ever climb out? I don't deserve it. Weakened by my own lies, I could not give life. So I should stay right here where I am, in this nightmare, allowing it to consume me until I no longer am," I concluded and closed the journal.

CHAPTER 20
Ashes and Rebirth

The smell of oranges and the Mediterranean Sea filled the air at the Airbnb I rented in Madrid for a business trip. Someone had just cleaned and left all the windows open, so the city's sounds could pierce my entire being. I closed my eyes to the silence. I loved being alone and far away. In late October, when the warm wind brought showers of colorful leaves all over the city, I would walk the streets for hours just to bathe in the feeling of my second favorite season in Spain after the blossoming spring.

Time did not allow for such things. The conference I came for started in two hours, and the ride to the IBM headquarters from Fuencarral took more than one hour. I unpacked, took a quick shower, made myself presentable, and took a cab to the marketing conference—the main reason I was there.

After I lost the pregnancy, I drowned myself in work, which paid off professionally.

For three days, I attended eight hours of conversations about the future of Marketing at IBM and two to three hours of conversations about nothing, with people I didn't know, during receptions. I kept my back straight, my face warm and sturdy, and showed my teeth to all the leaders who wanted to get to know the "pipes" of IBM—the Romanians working from the center in Bucharest. I didn't mind the fake of it all and could go along with anything. The real me came alive every evening, after hours, having a drink with my dear friend Aurelie, with whom I had lived in Plaza de España. My French sister, who is more Spanish than the Spaniards, had decided to move back to Madrid forever, while I lacked courage. The closest I could get was having this job designed to serve the Spanish market, which allowed me to travel to Madrid from time to time.

We loved to walk up and down Gran Via and find ice cream. Madrid is an amazing city for luxurious, posh experiences, where gorgeous models drink Moet for brunch, but it is also the best place for having ice cream from plastic cups while sitting on the curb in the sunny Plaza Mayor.

The sun was still high when we sat down, taking a break from walking to enjoy our ice-creams.

"Have you allowed yourself to mourn?" Aurelie asked me as I tried to break a frozen piece of Oreo between my teeth.

"Mourn?" I asked, looking surprised, trying to hold on to the lingering sweet taste disappearing from my mouth.

"Yes, you know what I mean. You act as if nothing happened when it did. You lost your first pregnancy. Have you allowed yourself to mourn?" she asked again.

"Women lose actual babies, while I only lost a pregnancy. There is nothing to mourn about," I answered, putting my plastic cup next to me, trying to fix my gaze on the pavement.

"So you did not. Rowena, if you don't give yourself permission to cry, to grow out of pain, who will? Are you waiting for someone to save you? Because no one will if you don't. I know you know better than this," she said, piercing my soul with her eyes.

I wanted to tell her she just unburied something in me, to let out all the pain I pushed away in a desperate scream, but all I could do was stare at a fixed point in front of me.

While staring, something happened, the entire noise of Plaza Mayor just stopped, and all I could hear was my breath. As if my breath became the only trace of myself.

It only lasted a split second, but right there and then something shifted in me. My mind stopped, and my self took control. I fell into her lap, my head on her left leg and both my hands surrounding her body. I hugged her with all my strength, and all the tears buried deep for months came out like a river breaking its dam. I could feel her caressing my hair from time to time. She didn't say anything. Any word would have hurt more.

Sunday morning, I decided to attend a catholic mass. It wasn't the beautiful choir or the words of the priest that got to me. It wasn't the feeling of taking off a heavy coat that brought the insight. A small painting showing an angel dying and rising to the sky caught my eye and did not let me look the other way.

I remember begging my father to stay when he took his last breath. I remembered Giovani, my beautiful nephew, and what was left of him in the coffin. I remembered the sound of silence as I waited to hear the baby's heartbeat. Everything came back to me in the form of a black box delivered and sitting on my right, on the bench under me.

"Should I carry this box with me?" I asked nobody, looking at the sculpted marble portraying Jesus.

"I want to leave it here," I said and got up, rushing to find the door.

The sun entering the small cracks of the massive wooden door surprised me. I tried to open it, and a terrible feeling to go back did not allow me to cross the gate. My body rushed back, beyond my control. I returned to the seat I was sitting on, closed my eyes, and took a deep breath.

"There is something else I cannot take with me," I said aloud to nobody.

"I will leave behind anything that does not serve the purpose I have here as a human being, not as a Gypsy, not as a woman, not as a Romanian. As a human. I allow all my labels to remain here, in this spot. I promise I will have the courage to become who I am." I added.

I got up, feeling light as a feather. When the wooden doors closed behind me, I knew I would never return. I smiled and made my way to my apartment. I had to pack to return to Romania.

The clouds over Bucharest were gorgeous. Sitting at the window seat on the Wizz Air flight, I could see all types of formations, each one more surprising than the next. I smiled at them as if they could see me. One, in particular, caught me because it had the shape of a human heart.

"I see you," I told the formation, just as I would do in my childhood.

"I forgot, for a while, to look at the sky. Now I remembered," I said quietly.

The taxi driver dropped me in front of my old gate. I took my luggage and sat on it, just looking at my street and my house.

Seeing it after many years of neglect, I could observe all the cracks in the outside paint. The old white windows we worked an entire summer to pay for were now too white, and the gate was too old to still be in use.

I got in, kissed my mother, and started writing in my journal. I wrote ten pages of what my ideal life would look like, in every little detail I could imagine, with no restrictions in thinking, just dreaming in the most authentic way. I could see myself traveling the world, having children, raising them as free spirits, moving far away, living in a beautiful home close to water and nature, and most importantly—finding true love—the unconditional love we all are searching for. It was dark when I finished writing, and I went to bed drunk with the images painted in my head. For some peculiar reason, I chose New York as the place to live. I had never been, I didn't know anyone living in the US, and I had no reason to choose this city over my beloved Madrid. Someone in me I didn't know well chose for me, and I surrendered to the dream I was now free to have.

CHAPTER 21

New York, New Me

It was a joy to come to work in the mornings and to see friends. I had already been working at IBM for a year and was building meaningful friendships with a few people, some of whom I worked with side by side. We would meet at the coffee shop close to the office from Monday to Friday at 8:30 a.m., where the baristas knew each of our preferences. The small group Cristina, Radu, and I created when we started in the same week in the company grew to include Adriana, Ioana, Alina, and many others, each character in the story with peculiarities one would never guess when you would first see us hanging out. And there we were, the Romani girl and the other strange people, looking normal when sipping our coffees.

On a hot September morning, after we arrived as a pack at our desks, at 9:00 a.m., my manager informed me she had some news and wanted to talk to me. Everyone's eyes turned to me while I followed her into a conference room, with my stomach still aching from the laughter we were sharing.

"I have some news for you, and sorry I had to be so serious back there. For now, we have to keep this between us," she said, her teeth now revealed as her eyes softened.

"Fine for me. Please spare me the emotions. Just tell me already what is happening," I said, my stomach now turned upside down.

"Well, we have selected you and three other colleagues of yours in this center to participate in an IBM Digital Marketing Conference held in New York," she announced.

My mind was somehow ready for this. I have dreamed of New York for months now, and I still could not believe the words this woman in front of me had just said.

"What do you mean?" I asked.

"Well, we selected you out of the two hundred people in the center, so you will get to participate in this conference where only IBM's top digital marketers worldwide are invited," she said.

"And you mean to tell me this is in New York? The New York from the US?" I asked.

"There is only one New York, and yes, that's where it is. Did you get the part where we selected you?" she tried to say.

"Yes," I interrupted.

I finally found some control over myself and said what she wanted to hear.

"I am sorry. Yes, I am extremely excited to attend this conference. It is such a great opportunity to learn," I finally said.

I had to go to the bathroom, close myself in a stall, and scream as hard as I could in my palms because I could not share the news with anyone yet. And it wasn't the trip itself that made me so happy, and it wasn't the fact I got to attend a conference with the best digital marketers at IBM that excited me. I cried tears of joy because I could see the power I had over creating my life in the way I wanted. This was my first real and absolute confirmation I could decide the journey I took because I had the steering wheel.

It rained cats and dogs when a few colleagues and I arrived at JFK Airport, where a shuttle was waiting to take us to the hotel. I couldn't see anything from the car window due to the heavy curtain of rain. We arrived at the hotel, where I got a room on the fifteenth floor. As soon as I got into the room, I opened the curtains, expecting to see the city. Instead, I saw more concrete, as the building across the street was even taller than mine. On the second day, in the morning, we went directly to IBM in Manhattan.

As soon as one walks into the New York City headquarters, a super-sized, red bunny made of stainless still awaits. The work of art is called *Balloon Rabbit*, and it is a fourteen-foot sculpture by Jeff Koons. Sad and tired faces of poorly paid guards tasked to check our bags every day adorned our entrance in Bucharest.

The conference meant eight hours of content and afternoon team activities every single day. Speakers from all over the world were teaching us the newest trends in digital marketing. IBM executives from different parts of the business would drive those learnings home by showing us how the company would move toward a digitalized world.

The only afternoon I could do some sightseeing was on Thursday—day four of the conference. Walking by myself on 5th Avenue, I finally had the chance to post some pictures on social media about this extravagant city. As soon as I did, a former ESCP colleague messaged me. Lewin was also visiting New York City during his layover toward his final destination—Brazil. We decided to hang out in the evening.

We had only gone out for drinks once in Madrid. Still, we both wanted to reconnect.

"Where do you want to go? I know zero about this Manhattan," I said.

"Let me take you to the Google office in New York. It's awesome, and I work there," he said.

I could not agree more.

The tour was grandiose. Each floor is themed and decorated. They had a special place dedicated to games and microkitchens with free snacks. The image of my sister and I arriving at Disney World after playing in the landfill across from our house on a hot summer day after I finished school is what came to my mind. At the end of the tour, my smile was up to my ears as if the kid inside me had just taken all the rides in the Disney Park.

"I want to work here," I said, surprising myself.

"Well, you can. Let me refer you," he said.

"I will definitely take you up on it," I said, trying to look composed.

At the conference, I soaked up all the valuable information given to us, hoping to capitalize on it to grow my career. I met some extraordinary IBMers who inspired me to want to someday level up to their standards.

One of them particularly impressed me with his passion for his work and helping others grow. Roger, fairly new to IBM, got hired to bring a new perspective: the one of the start-up community, as he led the "Start-up Weekend" movement in New York. Since the same type of event landed me my first job in Madrid, I shared the same passion for this community. It surprised me to see this huge corporation willingly challenging its own ways by bringing in people like Roger to show them a new way of doing things. A part of me had always been conflicted about corporations, thinking I could have much more impact in start-ups. This guy showed us how these two different worlds could blend.

He and I continued talking about our shared passion after the conference and decided to have a coffee on Saturday morning, my last full day in New York. He chose Blue Bottle, an independent coffee shop, somewhere close to Madison Square Garden, around 10:00 a.m. In my life so far, I never had a better coffee or such a passionate conversation with a man other than my two brothers. As he spoke about Start-up

Weekend, IBM, and his work as a teacher, I shared about my NGO—Women Manifesto, my former business cofounded with fellow IBMers, my ethnicity, and the hardship of trying to make it as a Romani woman in a business world, a part of me detached from the conversation and became a fly on the wall. I could observe everything without hearing anything. Not an inch on my body moved, the nervous movement of my right lid stopped, and my eyes had a clarity and a light I was unfamiliar with. The coffee shop became extremely quiet, and although these two people were total strangers, there was a feeling of absolute familiarity that both of them were trying to ignore.

I left the conversation thinking something in me changed, although I had no idea what. Now, looking back, I know for sure something changed radically. For the first time, I started believing that not all men are the same and that some are genuinely good people. Even if Roger was a stranger, he opened up this possibility in my mind.

The next day, a rainy Sunday afternoon, I flew back to Romania together with the colleagues I arrived with.

As soon as I arrived home, I wrote in my journal, "I am not the same person anymore, finally!"

Monday, jet-lagged and surprisingly energetic, I decided to take half a day off and work on my resume, at a coffee shop, in the hope of having a good chance for a job at Google. Roger and I started texting about the coffee shop scene in Bucharest, and he even helped me with some ideas about what to add or not to my CV. As soon as I had it in a good place, I hired a designer to make it look nice, and I sent it to Lewin. I got the call to schedule my interview for Google for a sales role in Dublin a few weeks after.

I spent October and November of 2016 mostly studying the art of interviewing for Google, as they had scheduled me for December. I cannot recall spending my afternoons or weekends doing anything else but reading about the company's culture and the possible questions. In early December, they flew me into Dublin for a three hour long interviewing process with three different people. I returned home, certain of failure.

It was foggy on a cold evening in December when my cousin Casandra asked me to drive to her place because we hadn't seen each other for weeks. I was almost on her street when I received a call from Dublin. I pulled over and answered.

"Is this Rowena Marin?" the voice asked.

"Yes," I said.

"Oh great, this is Ashley, calling from Google Dublin. Do you have a minute?" Ashley asked.

"Yes," I said.

"Awesome, I am calling to deliver the news," she continued.

"Yes," I said.

"If you accept, we want you to start your new role, in Dublin, on February 6," I thought she said.

"Wait, what? Do you mean I got into Google?" I asked.

"Indeed, you nailed the interviews, everybody spoke highly of you in their feedback, so if you want us, we want you," she said.

"Could you please double-check? This is Rowena Marin from Romania," I said.

"Yes, from Romania, Rowena Giorgiana Marin. It is you we want," she said.

I gently put the call on mute and screamed from the top of my lungs, "Yes, I made it!"

Ashley kept on asking, "Are you there?"

After a few minutes, I pulled myself together. "Ashley, thank you very much. I am excited to start. What are the next steps?" I asked.

I could not go to see Casandra. I stayed in the car for more than an hour, thinking about the next steps in my life. I was going to move again, and this time I wanted to leave everything behind. I wanted a fresh start where I got to truly create my own journey, from scratch. As I reflected on what I had to do to make this happen, tears were falling from my eyes, and I didn't do anything to stop them. Right there and then, I allowed myself to experience the happiness, sadness, pain, hope, and the guilt.

All these feelings were there with me in my car, pulling me in different directions. After an hour of reflecting, I knew what I had to do, and I knew no one could stop me now.

Christmas was close, so I gave myself the week to spend it with my family without rocking any boats. I visited all my cousins and even attended one last wedding, where I finally danced all night. No one else suspected I was saying goodbye to all of them in my heart.

It wasn't the ending with my people that got to me, nor the fear of the unknown. It was the feeling of guilt for leaving my mother behind again. Up to that point, my duty to her was more important than my life trajectory, as she made sure to raise me in that way. Seeing her unhappy because of me, even for the smallest thing, would trigger me in ways no one and nothing else could. So this moment when I knew I was failing her in the most profound way possible by leaving her alone could have been the biggest obstacle in my path to a new life.

I sat down with her on a cold January evening after coming from work and said, "Google accepted me for a role, Mom, and it is in Dublin." My sight was on the ground, regardless of how much I tried to look at her.

"Google, you mean the big company your brother kept talking about?" she said, lighting her big cigarette.

"Yeah, the big company," I said.

"And, do you want to take it?" she asked, searching for eye contact.

"It is a wild dream, of course. Still, there is nothing I want more," I said.

"How about Bogdan? Is he going with you?" she asked.

"No, the last breakup is the last one, Mom. I really cannot do it anymore, and you can see it." I said.

"Will going away make you happy?" she asked.

"It is a chance for me to start a new life, Mom. I want a new life. The life you never gave yourself because you decided you were more a Gypsy than a woman because you had my brothers when you were twenty-three, and my dad was sick most of the time. A life free from the heaviness of our ethnicity, a life completely and utterly mine," I said, now searching for her eyes.

Buna (Mom) & Rowena

She lit up a new cigarette and pulled one of her legs underneath her. The silence made my back hurt.

"Then do what you have to do. Go live. I will manage," she said, her chin now trembling.

I decided to make tea. I poured some for both of us, and we watched a soap opera together.

A few weeks later, I said goodbye to IBM and moved to Dublin with one small suitcase.

"Who am I? I don't know, but I now am free to find out and to define," I wrote in my journal while landing in Ireland.

Google offers one month of free housing when someone relocates to a new country for work. I got placed in a two-bedroom apartment with a large living room and big windows overlooking the river. Also, the company matched me with the best roommate one could wish for—Angela Esteve—a Spanish girl, taller than me and with a smile that made me feel at home around her. After the corporate housing time ended, we moved in together and lived as sisters for more than four years. We built a relationship that is still lasting, even if we moved to different continents.

I lived in Ireland for more than four years while I traveled the world, learned, grew, and fell in love. Roger, the man I met in New York, visited IBM Ireland the same year I moved to Dublin, and we started a long-distance relationship. Although so far from each other, as of 2018, we made a rule to see each other every other month, either in our respective countries, during our business travels, or on vacations. I never believed in soulmates, but what Roger and I have is as close as I got to this concept.

When you follow your inner voice and stay true to yourself, life flows easier, and you find answers. When you oppose this inner guidance to comply with other people's rules, life keeps on being difficult.

We got married in 2021, and as of then, we live in the US.

All the pieces fell into place, and I became Rowena, a woman I admire while leaving behind Rowi, the girl who did not know who she was.

Rowena - New York

PART FOUR
CHOICES

CHAPTER 22

On the Train Back to Baia Mare

Once every few years, I travel back to Baia Mare, the place where I was born. The city is constantly changing. Still, in many ways, it remains the same. They haven't changed the trains or tracks, so it can take me ten hours to cross our tiny country every time. It used to take the same amount of time when my father and I would go back and forth to Bucharest.

On the train, I sat by the window, watching the little snow-flakes, each looking like diamonds, picking up speed every other minute, falling as if the freedom to fall was their last wish. Between the moments of free fall, they would fly peace-fully, taking their time to dance a little before death. I knew their game so well because of all the long winters I spent in this part of the country.

As the train carried me away, I imagined the days of summer when my sister and I would rush to the swings on the banks of the Săsar river and come back home covered in dust, our nails black, our stomachs empty and with our smiles always up to our ears.

We were dancing like my friends, the snowflakes, taking our time before we became, before we had to choose: A disgrace to the people who raised us or a disgrace to our own self?

Your self: the part of you that is the most authentic, most connected to your soul, the real you.

Back then, the idea of even having a self was as from us as Zanzibar is from Baia Mare. Our concerns, as a community, revolved around needs like building tunnels through the mountains of snow to make our way into the empty flea markets. The constant struggle to survive from one day to the next prevailed in our lives. I've seen the eyes of the elders in their sixties, who had already given up on life, tired of its burden. I've also seen what a community can mean for those in need, how an open door and a warm meal can mean everything. I project those memories onto the train window, allowing the fall of the snowflakes to sink me back into the waters of my childhood.

It wasn't the vulnerability that crushed me every time I went back. It wasn't the lack of landmarks brought by the change of the city or the strange feeling of not belonging anywhere. I was a Gypsy in a racist country and a disgrace to my Gypsies. This was my reality, so I had to find a way of being in this world. My community had a pattern for the way I should live my life, and then this nagging voice inside of me just didn't allow it.

"You will regret this to the day you die," is what an aunt, who is now dead, told me when I decided to leave everything behind and move to Dublin. "Women maintain the household. They give their life for others. You? You are selfish," she said.

The internal battle between wanting to belong and wanting to know oneself is like the war in the *Mahābhārata*, where Arjuna, who is the leader of the Pandava army, questions if he should even engage in battle with the Kaurava army, as they are all his relatives. It is only by divine intervention he understands the reason why he must fight and win, as this is the main purpose of his life. I did not know any of this at the begging of my journey, but I guided myself from the inside, and it made all the difference.

In Baia Mare, our little apartment in the shabby building is still there, with the exact same balcony bar. Remembering it, I drew inward as the vulnerability and feeling of helplessness prevailing during those times came back like a river rushing to find the ocean. I can smell the frozen windows where I would spend hours waiting on the days we knew my mom would return home from her long trips to Hungary. I can see the bed where my dad used to sleep and where I would sneak in to watch over his breath. I can almost touch my two brothers' smiles when they returned from the flea markets to brighten up everyone with their good news. And I can feel my aunt's and uncle's love that would always bring me something small when they would sleep over on their way to different cities of the country.

This love we had for each other and unconditional support is what, for a long time, made me doubt if I should engage in any battle.

"Why go against your own people? Why not stay? Why not comply with the rules? Why not indulge in the ease of familiarity? Why would I ever want to disgrace the community which gave me the gift of knowing what love is?" These are the questions I carried with me for many years and refused to look at because of the depth of the answer.

But when you smell death from so close, as if it would be your own perfume, like we all did when my nephew died, you cannot ignore the absolute truth of a limited life. This perspective is what pushed me to see why engaging in this battle of life is what will give it meaning.

Also, asking my mother the question, "When was the last time when you were happy, when you felt truly alive?" and learning how long it had been since she experienced joy made me truly understand where the road of familiarity can take me.

In our community, there is a mighty woman raised only by her grandmother, who married a man she loved when she was young. I was very fond of her because she was always so positive, hard-working, and full of energy. Although she had no formal education, she has knowledge in literature, numbers, and facts about cities and countries in the world. Always curious, always willing to learn, and playful with all the children.

Since I have a real issue with memorizing names, I always called her Auntie. One day, because I had to create the list of guests to the party for my unofficial marriage, I needed her actual name. As I could not remember it, as much as I tried, and I could not write Auntie because I had dozens of aunts, I had to write the second way I used to refer to her in my private conversations: "The one who gets badly beaten by her husband." When I showed the list to my cousin Ramona, she knew who I was referring to.

This woman would disappear for weeks or even months, hospitalized or recovering after what her husband would do to her. Nobody intervened, nobody said anything, because he was her husband, and he could do whatever he wanted to.

They would sometimes say, "He is jealous because he loves her too much."

The couple is still together, and they have a son who, I heard, behaves the same way his father did with the girls he dates.

In a conversation with an older cousin of mine, I asked, "Why does she stay? One day he could kill her."

"Because we are Gypsies, Rowena. What do you want her to do? Get another husband?" she asked me back.

I did not answer because I knew what a sin this was in my community.

Sometimes the people we love most harm us in ways nobody else can. Sometimes we need to question even love to make sure it does not hinder our freedom to grow as human beings. Sometimes being a disgrace to people we love is better than being a disgrace to our self.

This is what I found on my journey through life once I decided it was worth it to "know thyself."

Still, on the train, I opened my eyes as we were crossing the Bistrita river, now a marvel of frozen water. The snowflakes were almost motionless. Watching, my heart skipped a beat.

I felt something close to joy, and I shut off any thoughts. I was just there and then, on that warm train, with my snow-flakes, going back to where it all started, so I always remain connected to my roots while I continue to grow.

CHAPTER 23

A Message to Kneeling Women

You have read my story, the stories of women in my family, and got a glimpse into my community's way. I hope you take this message to heart. Knowing who you are is what will tame the fire burning you from the inside.

At eight years old, I wrote a poem. My cousin, age nine, found it and read it out loud.

She tore the piece of paper in front of me and said, "This is not who we are!"

A Romani girl sells on the streets with the family, helps out at home with cleaning and raising the smaller children, and plays in the dirt with the other Gypsy kids. She doesn't write poems.

We live in a world in which we are theoretically free, but "How free are you?" is what I want to ask you.

Freedom implies no constraints in our growth as human beings, mentally, physically, and spiritually. With the weight of our ethnicity, that is our identity in a world that doesn't know us, and with the rules we are born into in our communities, I would ask, "Do you know who you are?"

I asked my seventy-three-year-old mother when was the last time she was happy. After a few superficial answers, her eyes lit up when she remembered the first year of marriage with my father, when she was twenty-two before the hardship of the life of a woman broke her down. Watching her giving up on life for many years breaks me, and I wonder what her life would be if she had allowed herself to know herself and live by her own rules. Although she has four children who love her more than life, it's not enough. The most important person who should love her is herself, and she does not.

Considering this, I changed the course of my life when I turned twenty-five. I found the courage to ask myself the tough questions to prevent being where she is now: waiting for this life to be over.

There were always breadcrumbs left by the real me, the curious spirit with no ethnicity or gender, the part of me which wanted to explore. It would come out to play when my father would read from his big books, my grandmother would tell one of her stories, or when my brothers would talk about their lives traveling.

Now, looking back, I understand I should have listened to this tiny little voice more carefully, although the noise around me was deafening. I hope you, my reader, will know better and will allow yourself to be guided by your real self through the good and the bad. This authentic inner voice is the only one with truthful authority and no one else. The journey to knowing this part of you is a hidden path through steep mountains, and it is the only one worth taking wholeheartedly. This path is sometimes lonely and painful, but if you look very carefully, the people who made an impact in this world, the ones who lived a fulfilled life, were not social butterflies. Sometimes our best friend is our own self once we truly commit to the journey.

A commonality among several world religions is the theory that feelings are rooted in two emotions: fear and love. In fear, the human is captive; lives a hard life, with shortages, full of trouble, and perpetual crisis. Although the living conditions might be similar, in love, the human being is open, sympathetic, reasonable, and finds solutions to hardships. I left fear behind. I understand who I am and what my soul wants because I stopped lying to myself by saying *I'm fine.*

Now I'm in a state of observing the world, of exploring the possibilities, in which the Romani, the woman, the Romanian, and all the other identities living within me are all in my toolbox. I don't allow anybody around me to dictate my decisions. I make decisions guided by intuition and love, and I use the necessary tools depending on the context. This sort of life is lived at its fullest, with courage and hope. I wish for every girl and woman to have the chance to live this way. A life lived every day.

So, I would tell you: your only purpose in this world should be your self-discovery. Who's your true self? What are your passions? What brings you joy? What makes your heart sing? What makes you wake up with a smile on your face?

You don't owe anything to anyone, not your mother, your father, your family, your husband if you're already married, or even your kids if you already have kids. I know this thought sounds extremely selfish and scary. Still, hear me out. If you wake up with a soul full of joy, the whole world will light up. Your kids, your husband, your parents, along with the rest of the world will be better because you are better. Continuing to live up to their expectations and ignoring your own self will be the death of your soul, your death as a woman. When your soul dies, you cannot make the world light up. The end of this road is becoming like the aunt who you know or hear about and whom nobody wants to be around.

Or like the love of my life: my mother, who lost her *self* to the rules of others.

No matter how naturally it comes to you to do what others expect of you, don't do it blindly. Listen and judge using your own intuition.

Think about what you want to do and make steps toward your goal, even if it hurts. Sometimes, the right path doesn't always feel natural and easy. And if this means you have to break the most serious rules, do it, as long as you stay true to your heart.

Listen to your soul with great consideration, don't rush things, ask women who engage in such journeys, and when you hear your heart telling the truth, act. It takes courage to fight the fear, whispering continuously to stay where we are and not explore 'dangerous' territories. But you are brave, even if you don't see it. Take the leap of faith and adventure into the most difficult journey: from mind to heart, from fear to love.

Take your courage, wear it like a second skin, and dare to become who you really are.

Rowena - First day at school

Acknowledgments

They say it takes a village to raise a child. In writing this book, it took many years and a village.

First, thank you, Dad, for teaching me to love stories when I was a kid.

Although I needed decades to heal from your loss before I was able to come back to this love you inspired in me, once I did, I gave birth to my star. Like Nietzche said, "You need to have chaos and frenzy in yourself to give birth to a dancing star." Your loss gave me the chaos, and later, I found the frenzy.

To my two brothers Raymond and Lucian, for their support in writing this book and unshaken love for me. Both of you had a tremendous impact on the way my story shaped. While reading parts of the manuscript as it unfolded, you offered perspectives I would not have been able to see. The basis of the book's first part and part of the second is my childhood memories, so integrating your take on what we lived together offers the readers the true experience. Also, thank you for providing me with the deep emotional support I needed to see this journey through.

To my husband for being curious and willing to learn about my culture and our ways. Thank you for being a true partner in anything I create and for your unconditional love and support.

Many thanks to the women that guided my journey to becoming an author: *Elena Stancu*—who encouraged me to write and introduced me to the magazine that published my first essay. *Cécile Barlier*—author of *The Gypsy's Book of Revelation*, for accepting to be my mentor in writing the first drafts of my stories. *Michele Herman*—my teacher at The Writer's Studio who had the patience to see me struggle. *Pamela Bergin and Jennifer Lewis*—my colleagues who were so nice not to cut my wings as I was learning to write in English and reviewed my work seeing only the potential in it.

Finally, thank you to everyone who believed in this book before it was a book, when it was just an idea. Thank you very much to everyone who provided feedback on the early drafts of my manuscript. I'm so grateful for your help in making this book the best it can be. A special thank you to everyone who preordered a copy of my book and donated to my prelaunch campaign. Thank you very much for reminding me that there are so many people in my communities who love and care about me.

Cătalina Posea	Oana Bajka
Theodor Manolache*	Elisa Jimenez Perez
Michele Sender	Salomé Peralta
Teodora Pătrăuceanu	Angela Esteve Lleches

Eugenia Nartea

Mădălina Spătaru

Clement Haeck

Ramona Ghica

Pablo Crespo

Thomas Casteran

Lisa DeAngelis

Eduardo Martin

Liliana Martin

Camelia Badea

Sara Carabantes

Diana Memic

Ana Pădurariu

Lenka Zounkova

Daniela Servi

Justin Mann

Reka Nagy

Victor Preda

Sireesha Baljepalli

Phu Truong

Joseph Maciariello

Lucian Marin

Bernie Milan

Adriana Maria Oncioiu

Lewin Keller

Florin Pravai

Maria Stroe

Nicoleta Chirică

Cristina Ailoae

Roxana Angheloiu

Diana Olar

Stephanie Miller

Paul Limbrey

Kanika Anand

Loredana Lavric

Arthur Török

Oana Dumitrescu

Melissa Milgate

Laila Alina Monterey

Mihaela Ciaușu

Anca Sercău

Irina Pocovnicu

Bruno Posa

Sylwia Prybicho

Paul Sharkey

Laura Cruceru

Aneta Pleşa

Maria Cristina Banu

Ioana Iliescu

Cristian Scrieciu

Kamar Thomas

Mădălina Pangrate

Federico Reyes

Cristina Feather

Neha Dakwala Shah*

Bogdan Droma

Lexi Bellas*

Jorge Lopez

Iveta Dobreva

Efrén López Arias

Andreea Simulescu

Mădălina Dumitrescu

Cristiana Grigore

Aurelie Sechet

Shraddha Shah

Ana Velicaru

Maja Bilic

Cristina Pînzari

Margareta Matache

Mari Kornhauser

Laura Vasile

Eric Koester

Ela Moraru*

Carmen Pungă*

Leia Tătucu

Andreea Agachi

Silvia Brinker

Dan Oros

Magda Slack

Ştefania Camelia Grosu

Narcisa Toderas-Alexa

Octavia Veresteanu

Arina Stoenescu

Daria Glaessgen

Tudor Papazoglu

Elena Stancu

Laura Ştefanescu

Melissa Escobar

Oana Cătalina Chircu

Cristina Slovacek

Laura Sorodoc

Andreea Balaianu

Georgeta Dumont

Alexandra Banu

Denis Blidariu

Horațiu Rotar

Alkistis Maria Michailidou

Gratiela Constantin

Andreea Bota

Fundatia Roma Education
Fund Romania*

Raymond Marin

Alexandra Untu Mueses

Diana Jianu

Anna Price

Mauli Delaney

Adrian Arauzo Vaillo

Dre Cetra

Ana Maria Petcu

Larisa Tiganetea

Cristina Marin

Raluca Cimpoiașu

Shiri Hergass

Jose Bustillo

Luisa Osorio

Clara Arghirescu

Elvira De la Cuesta

Yulino Osorio

Ana Aramă

Iulian Ghiocel

Minnie Vazquez

Kelly Pereira

Jane Simon

James Kennedy

Christopher Klug

Maria Stoian

Delia Marinescu

Leona Kindermann

Michelle Chernack

* = extra donations or multiple copies purchased

Printed in Great Britain
by Amazon

38531537R00129